The Gospel and Epistles of John

A Concise Commentary

Raymond E. Brown, S.S.
Union Theological Seminary
New York City 10027

1988

 THE LITURGICAL PRESS
Collegeville, Minnesota 56321

In 1960 an early form of Raymond E. Brown's introduction and commentary on the "Confraternity" translation of the Gospel and Epistles of John (a translation from the Latin) was published as #13 of The Liturgical Press *New Testament Reading Guide,* with minor revisions made in 1965 (2d ed.) and 1982 (3d ed.). That work has now been thoroughly revised, updated, and adjusted to the New American Bible 1986 translation of the New Testament, which appears at the top of each commentary page. Thus, this constitutes virtually a new work.

The reader is encouraged to use diligently the column of references found at the side of each commentary page as an important study tool. For those who wish to proceed to a greater depth in the study of these Johannine writings, Raymond E. Brown is the author of long commentaries in the Doubleday Anchor Bible series on *The Gospel according to John* (2 vols., #29 and 29A) and *The Epistles of John* (#30). An overall survey of Johannine thought and development is supplied by his book *The Community of the Beloved Disciple* (New York: Paulist, 1979).

Revised New Testament:

Scripture texts used in this work are taken from the Revised New Testament—New American Bible, © 1986 Confraternity of Christian Doctrine. All Rights Reserved. No part of the Revised New Testament—New American Bible may be reproduced in any form without permission in writing from the copyright owner.

Nihil obstat: Stephen J. Hartdegen, O.F.M., L.S.S., *Censor deputatus.*

Imprimatur: ✚ James A. Hickey, S.T.D., J.C.D., Archbishop of Washington. August 27, 1986.

Commentary:

Nihil obstat: Robert C. Harren, J.C.L., *Censor deputatus.*

Imprimatur: ✚ Jerome Hanus, O.S.B., Bishop of St. Cloud. March 9, 1988.

Copyright © 1988 by The Order of St. Benedict, Inc., Collegeville, Minnesota. All rights reserved. Printed in the United States of America.

Cover:

St. John the Evangelist from The Metropolitan Museum of Art, The Cloisters Collection, 1977. Used by permission. Cover design by Ann Blattner.

1   2   3   4   5   6   7   8   9

Library of Congress Cataloging-in-Publication Data

Brown, Raymond Edward.

    The Gospel and Epistles of John : a concise commentary / Raymond E. Brown.

      p.   cm.

    ISBN 0-8146-1283-0 (pbk.)

    1. Bible. N.T. John—Commentaries. 2. Bible. N.T. Epistles of John—Commentaries. I. Title.

BS2601.B77 1988   88-9622

226'.5077—dc19   —dc   CIP

CONTENTS

ABBREVIATIONS

Gn—Genesis
Ex—Exodus
Lv—Leviticus
Nm—Numbers
Dt—Deuteronomy
Jos—Joshua
Jg—Judges
Ruth—Ruth
1 S—1 Samuel
2 S—2 Samuel
1 K—1 Kings
2 K—2 Kings
1 Chr—1 Chronicles
2 Chr—2 Chronicles
Ezr—Ezra
Neh—Nehemiah
Tob—Tobit
Jud—Judith
Est—Esther
Jb—Job
Ps—Psalms
Prv—Proverbs
Qoh—Qoheleth
Ct—Canticles
Wis—Wisdom

Sir—Sirach
Is—Isaiah
Jer—Jeremiah
Lam—Lamentations
Bar—Baruch
Ez—Ezekiel
Dn—Daniel
Hos—Hosea
Jl—Joel
Amos—Amos
Ob—Obadiah
Jon—Jonah
Mi—Micah
Na—Nahum
Hb—Habakkuk
Zeph—Zephaniah
Hg—Haggai
Za—Zechariah
Mal—Malachi
1 Mac—1 Maccabees
2 Mac—2 Maccabees
Mt—Matthew
Mk—Mark
Lk—Luke
Jn—John

Acts—Acts
Rom—Romans
1 Cor—1 Corinthians
2 Cor—2 Corinthians
Gal—Galatians
Eph—Ephesians
Phil—Philippians
Col—Colossians
1 Th—1 Thessalonians
2 Th—2 Thessalonians
1 Tim—1 Timothy
2 Tim—2 Timothy
Tit—Titus
Phm—Philemon
Heb—Hebrews
Jas—James
1 Pt—1 Peter
2 Pt—2 Peter
1 Jn—1 John
2 Jn—2 John
3 Jn—3 John
Jude—Jude
Ap—Apocalypse
(Revelation)

1QS—the community rule of the Essenes who wrote the Dead Sea Scrolls

Hen—the apocryphal book of *Henoch* or *1 Enoch* (second century B.C.)

Test Jos—the *Testament of Joseph,* one of the apocryphal *Testaments of the Twelve Patriarchs* (probably B.C.)

Ant—the Antiquities of the Jews, a history by Josephus, first century A.D.)

DBS—the collection of dogmatic pronouncements of the Church edited by Denzinger-Bannwart-Schönmetzer (some texts in John have been mentioned therein)

NAB—*The New American Bible* 1986 translation of the New Testament, given at the top of the pages

Cf.—a reference to a discussion on a previous page

c.—chapter

v.—verse

Note: The verse numbers in Psalm references are according to the enumeration given in the Hebrew standard text, an enumeration followed in most translations except the King James Version and its revisions, which frequently run one verse *behind* the Hebrew verse number. Thus, the reference to Ps 69:10 on p. 30 below would be found in the Revised Standard Version at 69:9.

The Gospel According to John

Introduction

Text of the Fourth Gospel

In recent years much work has been done toward establishing the original Greek text of the Gospel of John. Codex Vaticanus is usually considered to have the best text; but two other famous codices, Sinaiticus and Bezae, often agree on a reading not in Vaticanus (especially in the first seven chapters) and may supply a more original text for a particular verse. These codices all date from the fourth and fifth centuries. Two recently discovered papyri of John (Bodmer—P[66]; P[75]) date from ca. A.D. 200; P[66] shows similarities to both Vaticanus and Sinaiticus/Bezae; P[75] is very close to Vaticanus.

In some verses the text of John may originally have been more concise than the form we know in the Greek manuscripts. Here quotations from John in the Fathers and the ancient translations, like the Syriac, are of help. There was a tendency on the part of the transmitter of a text to add an occasional explanatory phrase to a concise and sometimes obscure verse; in time this addition crept into the text of the manuscripts themselves.

Author

The Gospel calls attention to an eyewitness at the cross (19:35) who is the disciple whom Jesus loved (19:26). John 21:20, 24 claims that this anonymous beloved disciple both bears witness and "has written these things." St. Irenaeus (ca. A.D. 180) identified the disciple as John who lived at Ephesus till Trajan's time (ca. 98). (As a boy Irenaeus had known Polycarp, bishop of Smyrna, who is supposed to have known John.) This identification of the disciple-evangelist as John (son of Zebedee), with the minor variation that he had assistants, subsequently received almost universal church acceptance.

Today, it is recognized that such late second-century surmises about figures who had lived a century before were often simplified, and that authorship tradition was sometimes more concerned with the *authority* behind a biblical writing than with the physical writer. Accordingly it is doubted by most scholars that any one of the canonical Gospels was written by an eyewitness of the public ministry of Jesus, even though (as the Roman Catholic Church teaches) the Gospels are solidly rooted in oral traditions stemming from the companions of Jesus. The beloved disciple was one of the latter; but the contrast with Peter (13:23-26; 18:15-16; 20:1-10; 21:20-23) and his appearance at scenes where the Synoptic Gospels place none of the Twelve (19:26-27) suggest that he may not have been an apostle—a term never used in the Johannine Writings. The role of the beloved disciple was as a witness to Jesus and as the source of the Fourth Gospel tradition. This role would explain certain factors in the Gospel (which we shall continue to call "John," no matter who the beloved disciple and the evangelist were):

(a) *Familiarity with Palestine.* John knows the location of Bethany (11:1, 18), the garden across the winter-flowing Kidron (18:1), Solomon's porch in the Temple (10:23), the pool of Bethesda (5:2), the pool of Siloam (9:7), and the Lithostrotos (19:13). These sites are not mentioned in the other Gospels, and sometimes external evidence supports Johannine accuracy. Other Johannine geographical references (Bethany in 1:28; Aenon in 3:23) have not yet been identified, but we should be cautious about resorting to purely symbolic interpretations of the names.

(b) *Familiarity with Judaica.* Jewish feasts are mentioned in 5:10; 6:4; 7:2; and 10:22; and the ensuing dialogue shows a knowledge of festal ceremonies and theology. Jewish customs are mentioned both explicitly (purity regulations in 2:6; 19:28; paschal lamb in 19:36) and implicitly (makeup of the high priest's tunic in 19:24).

If the tradition behind John is firmly rooted in Palestine, the presentation of that tradition has moved considerably beyond Jesus' ministry. Indeed the evangelist acknowledges this (2:22) and defends such development as guided by the Spirit-paraclete (16:12-14). Christians have been expelled from the synagogue (9:22)—such a Jewish policy against the *minîm* or sectarians seems to have begun in the mid-80s and to have become more widely effective in the early 100s. Indeed, Christians have been killed by pious devotees of the synagogue (16:2). Consequently "the Jews" are a separate group from Christians, intensely disliked; and Jesus at times speaks as a non-Jew: "Written in *your* Law" (10:34); "In their Law" (15:25); "As I said to the Jews" (13:33). Unlike the Jesus of the Synoptic Gospels, the Johannine Jesus speaks explicitly of his divinity and his pre-existence (8:58; 10:30-38; 14:9; 17:5). He is hailed as God (20:28); and the basic argument with "the Jews" is not merely about his violation of the Sabbath rules but about his making himself equal to God (5:16-18). Traditional deeds of Jesus, like the multiplication of loaves and opening the eyes of the blind, have become the subject of long homilies involving theological reflection and debate along the lines of the Jewish interpretation of Scripture (5:30-47; 6:30-50; 9:26-34). Contrary to the Synoptic tradition, groups of Samaritans had come to believe in Jesus independently of Jesus' first followers (4:28-40).

Such development may be explained best if tradition about Jesus stemming from the beloved disciple has been reflected upon over many years and expanded in the light of Johannine community experiences. This tradition began with the acceptance of Jesus as the final prophet and the Messiah of Jewish expectations (1:40-49) but has gone beyond this to "greater things" (1:50). Jesus is not only the Son of Man who *will* come down from heaven at the end of time; the hour is already here and he has *already* come down from heaven. That is the secret of his ministry: what he says and does is what he saw when he was with God before the Word became flesh (5:19; 6:32-35). If the teachers of Israel believed Moses who claimed contact with God on Sinai and repeated what he heard there, Jesus is one who did not have to go to heaven but came from above where he saw God, so that whoever believes in him is never judged (3:10-21). It is tempting to speculate that the Samaritans catalyzed this view of Jesus as the descending Son of Man, a figure like but greater than Moses—significantly, the Jewish opponents of the Johannine Jesus considered him a Samaritan (8:48). The evangelist, who wove the theologically reflected tradition into a work of unique literary skill (p. 17 below), would presumably have been *a disciple* of the beloved disciple, about whom he writes in the third person. The beloved disciple would have lived through the historical development of the community (and perhaps through expulsion from the synagogue), and so there may have been a certain symbiosis between him and the Gospel that put on paper his tradition and experience and the reflection he shared.

The Johannine Writings

After the tradition came from the beloved disciple and after the body of the Gospel was written by the evangelist (sometime after the mid-80s), further editorial work seems to have been done. For instance, there are two endings to Part I of the Gospel, one in c. 10 and one in c. 12; and there are two endings of the Gospel, one in c. 20 and one in c. 21 (below, pp. 61, 100). Several speeches seem to be reported twice (p. 19). Most of this editing seems to be by way of addition (even when an addition is awkward—see Last Discourse, pp. 78-79) rather than by way of changing. Accordingly, scholars suspect that the editor was not the evangelist (who would have been freer to deal with his own work) but *a redactor* whose additions gave us the final form of the Gospel as we now know it. Presumably this was when the evangelist was no longer present and after the beloved disciple was dead—a deduction from the redactor's care in 21:23 to deny the thesis that the disciple would not die. The earliest Egyptian papyrus fragment (Rylands P[52]) of John (18:31-38) is dated ca. 135-150. If we allow time for the copying and spread of the Gospel to Egypt, John was certainly written before 125. Irenaeus' tradition spoke of Trajan's reign (98–117) for the Gospel. But one must allow for a long tradition, which began with the beloved disciple in Jesus' ministry, moved through years of oral preservation, community development, and possible earlier written collections (a book of Signs; see 20:30), before it was embodied in the evangelist's main composition (ca. A.D. 90), and came to the final form in the hands of the redactor (100–110). The redactor, writing after the angry division of the Community described in the Epistles (pp. 106–8 below), recognizes Peter's authority over Jesus' sheep (Jn 21:15-17). Thus he may be closer to the Diotrephes, criticized in 3 Jn 9–10 for assuming "first place" in a church, than to the author of 1 Jn 2:27, who denied the need for teachers.

Relation to the Synoptics

A comparison of the Fourth Gospel to the first three Gospels shows obvious differences. Peculiarities of the Fourth Gospel include: setting of much of the public ministry in Jerusalem rather than in Galilee; the significant absence of the kingdom of God motif (only in 3:3, 5); long discourses and dialogues rather than parables; only some seven miracles, including the unique Cana changing of water to wine, healing a man *born* blind, and the raising of Lazarus.

Yet there are also important similarities to the Synoptics, especially in beginning the ministry with John the Baptist and in the concluding narratives of the Passion and Empty Tomb. In particular, the closest similarities are with *Mark*, e.g., in the sequence of events in Jn 6 and Mk 6–8; and in such verbal details as "genuine nard of great value (?)" (Jn 12:3), 300 denarii (12:5), and 200 denarii (6:7). There are parallels, more of motif than of wording, with *Luke*, e.g., lack of a night trial before Caiaphas (Jn 18); the three "not guilty" statements in the Pilate trial (Jn 18–19); the miraculous draught of fishes (Jn 21). There are fewer similarities with *Matthew*; yet compare Jn 13:16 with Mt 10:24; and Jn 15:18-27 with Mt 10:18-25. The best overall solution is that, while the Synoptic Gospels represent one basic tradition about Jesus' deeds (with Mt and Lk drawing upon Mk), to which has been added (in Mt and Lk) a tradition of Jesus' sayings (Q), *John draws upon an independent and different tradition (or traditions) of Jesus' deeds and sayings.* Even if occasionally the Synoptic and Johannine traditions reproduce in variant forms the same deeds or sayings, there is no convincing evidence that the fourth *evangelist* knew the present form of the Synoptic Gospels, although he may have been aware of traditions incorporated later into Lk. The final Johannine *redactor* probably knew Mk.

The independent traditions that came down to the fourth evangelist (many of them originating with the beloved disciple) had circulated in the Johannine community for years, and so the Gospel assumes basic knowledge of the Jesus events. Accordingly, the evangelist is able to select a few choice incidents (one paralytic, in c. 5; one blind man, in c. 9; one raising from the dead, in c. 11) and dramatically arrange these selections to highlight the nature and mission of Jesus. His audience believes; he wishes to justify their faith in the divinity of Jesus by eyewitness testimony (20:30-31). The Synoptic tradition has the basic facts, but, for instance, crowds Jesus' self-revelation before the Jerusalem authorities into the Holy Week of a one-year public ministry. John shows that Jesus' activities at Jerusalem were spread over at least two years.

Again, we shall see in John a strong emphasis on events in Jesus' life which foreshadow the sacramental life of the church. John is dealing with a Christian audience which already depends on baptism for its life and the eucharist for nourishment of that life. The only information in the Synoptics on baptism is a verse commanding it (Mt 28:19), and on the eucharist, the verses instituting it (Mk 14:22-24). John never mentions these institutions (perhaps presupposing them), but gives the rich background and meaning of baptism in references to the living water of rebirth in cc. 3, 4, 7, 13, and of the eucharist in the discourse on the living bread in c. 6, and perhaps in references to the wine of the new dispensation in cc. 2, 15. John shows the ultimate source of both sacraments in 19:34. It is also John who gives us the clearest information on forgiving sins in 20:22-23.

The whole theological basis of the sacramental system is found in Johannine thought: the Word became flesh (1:14) to conquer the world of flesh or matter that had been placed under the power of Satan by human sin (1 Jn 5:19). Jesus conquered Satan (12:31; 16:33), but the working-out of that victory in time, the reconquest of the world of matter for Christ, is the work of the church (17:15-18; 1 Jn 5:4). And in that reconquest, by divine irony, the common things of this world, bread and water and wine, become the instruments of divine life in the sacraments (Jn 4:14; 6:52).

Thus, in summation, while the Fourth Gospel presupposes a Jesus tradition not unlike that of the Synoptics, it was not written to supplement lacunae in the previous Gospels. The Fourth Gospel presents an independent tradition with its own purpose and witness.

Sources of John's tradition

John is often characterized as a Hellenistic Gospel. The abstract ideas like light and truth; the dualistic division of humanity into light and darkness, truth and perversity; the concept of the Word—all of these were once held to be the product of Greek philosophical thought and the pagan mystery religions. Or (before the discovery of the early papyri) John was treated as a late second-century product of Gnosticism. Others have wandered farther afield, seeking the origins of John in Eastern sects, like the Mandeans. All of these theories agreed that the Johannine idiom of thought could not have stemmed from the Palestinian world of Jesus of Nazareth. Two discoveries of the 1940s have rudely shaken this maxim of radical criticism:

Dead Sea Scrolls

From the caves of Qumran, near the Dead Sea, have come manuscripts dating from Jesus' time and earlier—the library of the Essenes, one of the Jewish sects. And we find these documents full of the vocabulary that the critics once agreed was not authentically Palestinian, viz., a world divided into light and darkness (Jn 3:19-21); people under the power of the angel of darkness (1 Jn 5:19); people walking in light or in darkness (8:12; 1 Jn 1:5-7); walking in truth (2 Jn 4; 3 Jn 4); testing the spirits (1 Jn 4:1); the spirits of truth and perversity (1 Jn 4:6). The resemblance in vocabulary and thought between the Dead Sea Scrolls and John is truly startling, and should forever banish the idea that John is completely a product of the non-Jewish world. That these parallels exist in the three Johannine Epistles as well as in the Fourth Gospel is another argument for seeing the same ultimate source behind both.

There is no evidence for a *direct* familiarity of John with the Dead Sea Scrolls; rather it is a question of indirect acquaintance with a type of thought and expression current at Qumran, and perhaps in a much wider area. (There are interesting parallels between what we know of John the Baptist and the beliefs of these Qumran Essenes. Since the beloved disciple was probably a disciple of the Baptist, the latter may have been the channel of Qumran influence on John.) That much of this Johannine-Qumran vocabulary appears in the speeches of Jesus in John (to a much greater extent than in the Synoptics) need not lead us to conclude hastily that Jesus' speeches in John are the artificial compositions of the author. If Qumran is but an example of a wider range of thought, Jesus could well have been familiar with its vocabulary and ideas; for the Word-made-flesh spoke the language of his time. John, with a special affection for this style of thought, may have been more attentive in preserving it.

We admit, however, that this is not a complete solution to the problem of the Jesus of John who speaks very differently from the Jesus of the Synoptics. As we shall see in the commentary, however, even some of the most peculiarly Johannine expressions that we find on Jesus' lips do have a faint echo in the Synoptics (e.g., the "hour" in Mk 14:35; also #1 below). The Johannine tradition may be remembering and emphasizing ideas that did not seem important to the Synoptic writers. It could appeal to the Paraclete for the right to recall and develop in later years things that seemed trivial at an earlier date (14:26).

Gnostic documents from Nag Hammadi (Chenoboskion)

About the same time that the Dead Sea Scrolls were discovered, there was found at Chenoboskion in Egypt a Gnostic library. Hitherto, very few actual Gnostic works were known; our knowledge of second-century Gnosticism came from the reports of the Church Fathers. Even a cursory glance at these new documents shows a profound difference between them and John. The theory that John borrowed from such Gnosticism is implausible; more likely the second-century Gnostics drew from John, and not vice versa.

Sequence in John

Because of abrupt transitions between parts of John, many scholars have attempted to rearrange certain chapters (without any manuscript evidence), e.g., some would put c. 6 before c. 5 because c. 4 ends in Galilee where c. 6 begins, while all of c. 5 is in Jerusalem. Personally we see no need of this. John gives us a very schematic account of Jesus' ministry, and does not worry about transitions unless they are purposeful (e.g., the careful sequence of [seven?] days in cc. 1–2). In the series of feasts in cc. 2, 5, 6, 7 and 10 which serves as the framework for Jesus' ministry, little attention is paid to the intervals that separate the feasts (see 7:19; 10:26-27 below). Moving incidents around to get a better time-sequence is giving priority to something that was not of great import to the final editor who could scarcely have missed the obvious inconsistencies. Any theory that the pages of John were confused by chance is sheer imagination.

Plan of John

We maintain that in its main lines John follows a careful plan, but a Semitic plan, not a Western one. There are overlappings of themes that defy schematization. Several ideas are developed at the same time and our division will vary according to which idea we would emphasize. With this in mind, we shall not attempt a strict division, but only make suggestions for tracing ideas. In the present form of John, at least this general plan is clear:

1:1-18   THE PROLOGUE
                An introduction to and summary of the career of the incarnate Word.

PART ONE may be subdivided into four sections:
1. seven days of gradual revelation of Jesus (1:19–2:11)
2. themes in 2:1–4:54
   a) the replacement of Old Testament institutions:
   CANA—replacement of Jewish purifications (2:1-11)
   JERUSALEM—replacement of the Temple (2:13-25)
   NICODEMUS—replacement of birth into the Chosen People (3:1-36)
   SAMARITAN WOMAN—replacement of worship at Jerusalem (4:1-42)
   Second Cana Miracle closing the section (4:43-54)
   b) reaction to Jesus by individuals representing a class:
   OFFICIAL JUDAISM (at Jerusalem)
   Temple authorities (2:13-25)
   Nicodemus the Pharisee (3:1-36)
   SAMARITAN (4:1-42)
   ROYAL OFFICIAL (Galileans; 4:43-54)
3. themes in 5:1–10:42
   a) the replacement of Old Testament feasts:
   THE SABBATH—Jesus, the new Moses, replaces the Sabbath ordinance (5:1-47)
   PASSOVER—the Bread of Life (revelatory wisdom and the eucharist) replaces the manna (6:1-71)
   TABERNACLES—the Source of living water, the Light of the world, replaces the water and light ceremonies (7:1-10:21)
   DEDICATION—Jesus is consecrated in place of the Temple altar (10:22-42)
   b) the theme of *life* (begun in 2:1–4:54) is developed in 5:1–7:52; the theme of *light* is developed in 8:1–10:42 (particularly in the healing of the man born blind)

4. the Lazarus theme (11:1–12:36)

The raising to life of Lazarus leads directly to the condemnation of Jesus. Lazarus is present at the anointing of Jesus for burial (12:1-8), and enthusiasm over the miracle performed in his favor occasions the Palm Sunday scene (12:9-36). The raising of Lazarus is the culmination of the life-light themes.

PART TWO may be subdivided into three sections:
1. the Last Supper (13:1–17:26)
   a) the washing of the feet and the betrayal (13:1-30)
   b) Jesus' Last Discourse:
   Introduction (13:31-38)
   Part One (14:1-31; duplicated in 16:4-33)
   Part Two (15:1–16:3)
   Part Three (17:1-26)
2. Jesus' passion and death (18:1–19:42)
   a) the garden scene (18:1-12)
   b) inquiry before Annas; Peter's denial (18:12-27)
   c) trial before Pilate (18:28–19:16)
   d) crucifixion, death, and burial (19:17-42)
3. the resurrection, ascension, and conferring of the Holy Spirit (20:1-31)

Characteristics of the Fourth Gospel

Attention to the following literary characteristics will aid tremendously in understanding the Gospel according to John. In the commentary reference will be made to these stylistic devices by the presence of the sign # in the margin.

#1 MISUNDERSTANDING. Jesus frequently uses figurative language or metaphors to describe himself or to present his message. In an ensuing dialogue the questioner will misunderstand the figure or metaphor, and take only a verbal or material meaning. This allows Jesus to explain his thought more thoroughly and thereby to unfold his doctrine. Part of this may be a studied literary technique on the part of the author or of the earliest Christian catechesis. In a sense, too, these figures or metaphors are the Johannine equivalent of the Synoptic parables, for in John the kingdom of heaven stands in our midst in the person of Jesus. In the Synoptics the parables are frequently misunderstood, just as the metaphors are in John. (Cf. Jn 2:20; 3:4; 4:11; 6:26; 8:33; 11:11-12, 24; 14:5-8.)

#2 IRONY. The opponents of Jesus are given to making statements about him that are derogatory, sarcastic, incredulous or, at least, inadequate

17

in the sense that they intend. However, by way of irony these statements are often true or more meaningful in a sense that they do not realize. (Cf. Jn 3:2; 4:12; 6:42; 7:28-29, 35; 8:22; 9:24, 40; 11:48-50; 12:19; 19:3, 14, 22.)

#3 TWOFOLD MEANING:

a) there is often a play on various meanings of a given word that Jesus uses, meanings based on either Hebrew or Greek. (Cf. Jn 3:3, 8, 13, 17; 7:8; 13:1; 15:21; 19:30.)

b) In the Fourth Gospel the author frequently intends the reader to see several layers of meaning in the same narrative or in the same metaphor (figurative language). This is understandable if we think back to the circumstances in which the Gospel was composed: (1) There is a meaning that stems from the historical context in the life of Jesus. The audience that listened to Jesus and witnessed his actions would necessarily understand his words and analyze his works according to their own religious background and ways of thinking. We may call this the historical meaning of the passage. Yet there is a more profound meaning of Jesus' words and actions that would be seen by the believing Christian community. As the message of Jesus was preached and taught in the early church, as it was prayed over in the liturgy, all its implications would gradually unfold; and the Christians would come to understand much more of what Jesus had meant than did those who had first heard him in Galilee and Jerusalem. Sometimes it is a question of deeper insight into Jesus' mission, for instance, the realization that the Temple that he said would be destroyed and raised up in three days was his own body (Jn 2:20). Other times it is a question of understanding ideas about the church and the sacraments (especially about baptism and the eucharist). A community that had received these sacraments could see the profound meaning of Jesus' "living water" and "bread of life." See Jn 1:29, 31; 2:8, 20; 3:5; 4:11; 6:35-58; 9:7; 11:4; 13:1-17; 19:36. (2) Jesus is from another world, from above; yet he speaks the language of this world, from below. Inevitably those who meet him, whose experience is on the lower level, misunderstand his meaning from above when he speaks of water, bread, flesh, etc. Readers, while challenged to recognize a higher meaning, will also be puzzled by the stranger from above and so invited to believe.

#4 INCLUSION. John often mentions a detail (or makes an allusion) at the end of a section which matches a similar detail at the beginning of that section. This is a way of packaging sections by tying together the beginning and the end. (Cf. Jn 1:19, 28; 2:1, 4; 4:54; 9:41; 10:40; 11:40; 19:14-16, 36-37; 20:28; 21:13.)

#5 REALIZED ESCHATOLOGY. The Synoptics situate at the end of time such things as judgment, the return of Jesus, becoming sons of God (Mt 25:31; Lk 6:35; 20:35-36). John, without denying the truth of this, emphasizes that these things have already begun; his eschatology (doctrine of the last things) is in part already realized. (Cf. Jn 3:18; 5:24-25; 7:12; 9:16; 10:19-21; 12:31-33; 14:1-3, 18-20; 17:3.)

#6 DIALOGUE BECOMING MONOLOGUE. Jesus may begin a conversation with a given person or audience; yet as the speaking continues, the hearers fade away and at the end his words seem to have taken the character of a discourse in universal terms. Part of this may be the editorial combining of several speeches. The effect, however, is to free Jesus' words from the limitations of circumstance and to make them eternally and universally valid. (Cf. 3:16; 10:1-18; cc. 14–17.)

#7 DUPLICATE SPEECHES. Occasionally a speech of Jesus seems to say essentially the same thing as a speech already recorded, almost to the point of verse-to-verse correspondence. The solution we offer is that the speech had been presented on various occasions with minor variants. This could easily happen if the final Gospel redactor, finding in the Johannine tradition two different versions of the same topic, did not want to lose either version; and so, editing the Gospel after the evangelist died, he incorporated the second version at an appropriate place, often close to the first. Other times it may be a case of Jesus' words containing a twofold meaning; John draws attention to both by giving one sense in the first version and the other in the second. (Cf. Jn 3:31-36; 5:26-30; 6:51-58; 8:13-18; 10:7, 9 and 10:11, 14; 12:44-50; 13:1-30; 16:4-33.)

#8 REARRANGEMENT IN RELATION TO THE SYNOPTIC ORDER:

a) Events that are presented as units in the Synoptics are often found dismembered and dispersed in the Fourth Gospel. It is difficult to decide which situation is more original: the Synoptics may have assembled isolated features for the sake of a unified picture; or John may have distributed fragments of an original unit throughout the Gospel to show that the lesson of that unit was true during the whole of Jesus' life. Or we may have coincidental similarity between two distinct events (this simple solution is *not* always possible or feasible). (Cf. Jn 6:51-58, 67-69, 70-71; 10:24-25; 11:52; 12:27ff; 14:31; 18:1-12, 24.)

b) Occasionally the opposite is true: events that are a unit in John are found separated in the Synoptics. (Cf. Jn 1:38-49; 2:13-19; 11:1ff; 15:1ff.)

A Translation of the Prologue from the Greek in Poetic Format

[1]In the beginning was the Word;
the Word was in God's presence,
and the Word was God.

[2]He was present with God in the beginning.

[3]Through him all things came into being,
and apart from him not a thing came to be.

[4]That which came to be found life in him,
and this life was the light of the human race.

[5]The light shines on in the darkness,
for the darkness did not overcome it.

([6]Now there was sent by God a man named John [7]who came as a witness to testify to the light, so that through him all might believe—[8]but only to testify to the light, for he himself was not the light.)

[9]He was the real light
that gives light to everyone;
he was coming into the world.

[10]He was in the world,
and the world was made by him;
yet the world did not recognize him.

[11]To his own he came;
yet his own people did not accept him.

[12]But all those who did accept him,
he empowered to become God's children—
those who believe in his name,

[13]those who were begotten,
not by blood,
nor the flesh,
nor human desire,
but by God.

[14]And the Word became flesh
and made his dwelling among us.
And we have seen his glory,
the glory of an only Son coming from the Father,
rich in kindness and fidelity.

([15]John testified to him by proclaiming: "This is he of whom I said, 'The one who comes after me ranks ahead of me because he existed before me.'")

[16]And of his riches
we have all had a share—
kindness in place of kindness.

[17]For while the Law was a gift through Moses,
this kindness and fidelity came through Jesus Christ.

[18]No one has ever seen God;
it is God the only Son,
ever at the Father's side,
who has revealed him.

The Gospel According to John

Text and Commentary

1 ¹In the beginning was the Word,
and the Word was with God,
and the Word was God.
²He was in the beginning with God.

³All things came to be through him,
and without him nothing came to be.
What came to be ⁴through him was life,
and this life was the light of the human race;

THE PROLOGUE

Jn 1:1-18

The prologue is a hymn, a poetic summary of the whole theology and narrative of the Gospel, as well as an introduction. It can be fully understood only *after* the Gospel has been studied. (We ask readers to cover this section hastily at first, and then, after completing the Gospel and commentary to return for further study.) We shall mention frequently John's conception of a great cycle: *the Son descends from heaven to our level, and ascends back to heaven bringing us up with him to the divine level.* The prologue describes the Son in heaven and the descent; the Gospel describes the walking among us and the final elevation and return to the Father.

Genesis and the "Logos" doctrine—1:1-5

The first verses recall the Genesis account of creation. At the moment of creation the Word already existed. Uncreated, the Word was in the Father's presence; indeed the Word was God. What are the sources of the Johannine conception of the Son of God as the "Word"? First of all we may look to the Genesis account that tells how God created by simply saying, "Let there be. . . ." It was thus through God's *word* that things came into being. To this idea of God's creative word, we may join the concept of divine wisdom, which in pre-Christian thought became personified as a woman. Divine, and yet almost distinct from God, wisdom had a role in creation; she was sent forth from the mouth of God and helps to save human beings. In the *Word* of the prologue, we have a union of wisdom and

Gn 1:1-5

Ps 33:6;
Wis 9:1

Wis 7:25;
8:5; 9:9-11

Sir 1:1;
24:1-12

⁵the light shines in the darkness,
  and the darkness has not overcome it.
⁶A man named John was sent from God.
⁷He came for testimony, to testify to the
light, so that all might believe through
him. ⁸He was not the light, but came to
testify to the light. ⁹The true light, which

enlightens everyone, was coming into the
world.
¹⁰He was in the world,
  and the world came to be through
  him,
  but the world did not know him.
¹¹He came to what was his own,

God's word, a divine person uncreated and existing with the Father. `Ap 19:13`

3-4   Through the Word things were created, and separated from his activity not a thing can exist. Interestingly the phrase, "Without him nothing came to be," occurs verbally in the Dead Sea Scrolls. The last phrase in verse 3 should be read with verse 4 as: "That which came to be was [or found] life in him." The creative Word of God was the source of life as we read in Genesis. And if humanity would only have realized it, the life supplied by this Word was its light—the light given by God to walk in (remember that light was the first gift of creation). `Col 1:15-16` `1QS 11, 11` `Cf. p. 14` `Jn 8:12` `Gn 1:3`

5   John then makes tacit reference to human rejection of God's light through sin, and the introduction of the darkness of evil into God's creation. John stresses that this darkness did not conquer the light—the theme in Gn 3:15 of the ultimate victory of the woman's seed over the serpent.

John the Baptist—1:6-8

As an example of a ray of light still shining in the darkness, John presents the Baptist, who came to remind humanity of the light. These prosaic verses interrupt both the poetry and the consecutive thought of verses 5 and 9, and may originally have been elsewhere in the Gospel, perhaps before verse 19. Their place here now seems to show that for the final editor of the Gospel, verses 9ff refer to the *Incarnate* Word, Jesus. Other scholars make a case for seeing in verses 9-11 Old Testament events (creation and the covenant), and beginning the incarnation with verse 12. But the introduction of the Baptist, who prepared for Jesus, makes us think that verse 9 is intended to refer to Jesus. `Cf. p. 11` `Jn 1:23`

Rejection of the light—1:9-11

The first half of the Gospel (1:1–12:50) shows us the rejection of Jesus by the darkness (evil forces) and "the Jews." Verses 9-11 sum up that rejection. The true light of the world came into the world he had created; and the world, directed to `Jn 8:12; 9:5; 12:46; 3:19-20`

10

but his own people did not accept him.

¹²But to those who did accept him he gave power to become children of God, to those who believe in his name, ¹³who were born not by natural generation nor by human choice nor by a man's decision but of God.

¹⁴And the Word became flesh
and made his dwelling among us,
and we saw his glory,
the glory as of the Father's only Son,
full of grace and truth.
¹⁵John testified to him and cried out, saying, "This was he of whom I said, 'The one who is coming after me ranks ahead

11   evil by human sin, rejected him. He came to his own land, and the people that had been prepared for his coming by Moses and the prophets rejected him.

Jn 4:44;
5:39, 46

Acceptance of the light—1:12-13

Yet some did believe him: the second half of the Gospel deals with the salvation of these believers, the new "his own." These he enabled to become God's children. The Son would breathe his Spirit of new life on these as God breathed the spirit of life on Adam. There would be a new creation to replace the old which had rejected God. The believers are those whom the Father has given him, those predestined by a predestination that shows itself in doing the good work of God.

Is 55:10-11
Jn 13:1
Jn 3:5-6;
20:22
Gn 2:7
Ap 21:1
Jn 6:64-65;
10:26
Jn 3:21
1 Jn 2:29

13

A "New Covenant"—1:14-18

Just as a new creation replaces the old, a new covenant replaces the old covenant with Israel on Sinai, because the people who originally were his own rejected Jesus. A constant theme in the Gospel is Jesus' replacement of the institutions, Temple, and feasts of "the Jews." This is summed up poetically in verses 14-18. For the Word became flesh (flesh means human nature) and set up his Tabernacle in our midst ("made his dwelling among us"). One of the signs of God's pact with Israel on Sinai was the Tabernacle made in the desert. The Tabernacle and its later successor, the Temple, were the seat of divine presence among God's people, the seat of God's glory. In the new covenant, the humanity of the Word, his flesh, becomes the supreme localization of divine presence and glory.

Ex 25:8-9
Ex 40:34
1 K 8:10-
11, 27

The favorite description of the God who drew up the old covenant was that he was "rich in kindness and fidelity" (*kindness*: a technical term for God's mercy in choosing Israel out of all the nations as his people; *fidelity*: God's faithfulness to the promises he made Israel in the covenant). The same expression is used in v. 14 ("full of grace and truth") to characterize the God of the new covenant. (Once again the witness

Ex 34:6

15

of me because he existed before me.'"
¹⁶From his fullness we have all received, grace in place of grace, ¹⁷because while the law was given through Moses, grace and truth came through Jesus Christ. ¹⁸No one has ever seen God. The only Son, God, who is at the Father's side, has revealed him.

II: THE BOOK OF SIGNS
John the Baptist's Testimony to Himself.
¹⁹And this is the testimony of John. When the Jews from Jerusalem sent priests and Levites [to him] to ask him, "Who are you?" ²⁰he admitted and did not deny it, but admitted, "I am not the Messiah." ²¹So they asked him, "What are you then?

of the Baptist, too fervent to be kept silent, a duplicate of v. 30, breaks the connection between verses 14 and 16.) We are
16-17 the sharers in this new wealth of kindness ("grace") and fidelity, this new covenant replacing the old. The words of God, the ten commandments, were engraved in stone on Sinai for Moses as the expression of God's kindness in the old covenant. The Word of God is now engraved in the flesh of Jesus as the embodiment of God's kindness in the new covenant. God
18 would not let Moses see him in the Old Testament; now the Son who has known him from all eternity reveals him. The Gospel is the story of that revelation.

Jer
31:31-33

Ex
33:18-23

Jn 6:46;
14:8-10
Heb 1:1-2

PART ONE—THE BOOK OF SIGNS

Jn 1:19–12:50

Section 1. The First Week of the New Creation (1:19–2:12)

The Baptist witnesses before the Pharisees—1:19-28

The public appearances of Jesus open with the witness of John the Baptist to the paschal Lamb of God; his public appearances will close with the witness of the unnamed beloved disciple, as the paschal Lamb is dying on the cross on Passover eve. John gives us a triptych: the Lamb in the center and the two witnesses on either side.

Acts
1:21-22

Jn
19:35-36
#4

In the Synoptics we find hostility between John the Baptist
19 and the Jewish authorities but no open clash. In John "the Jews" (note: in John this term means those of Jewish birth who reject Jesus) are in direct attack from the very beginning. The whole of John is a trial of Jesus by the leaders of his people, and the Baptist is the first trial witness. The guardians of the national religion wish to know by what authority he baptizes. The an-
20-21 swers he gives about himself are negative; he becomes voluble only when talking about the One to follow him. He begins by denying he is the Messiah. In the Synoptics Jesus identifies John

Mt 3:7;
21:32

Mt 11:14;

Are you Elijah?" And he said, "I am not." "Are you the Prophet?" He answered, "No." ²²So they said to him, "Who are you, so we can give an answer to those who sent us? What do you have to say for yourself?" ²³He said:

"I am 'the voice of one crying out in the desert,

"Make straight the way of the Lord,"' as Isaiah the prophet said." ²⁴Some Pharisees were also sent. ²⁵They asked him, "Why then do you baptize if you are not the Messiah or Elijah or the Prophet?" ²⁶John answered them, "I baptize with water; but there is one among you whom you do not recognize, ²⁷the one who is coming after me, whose sandal strap I am not worthy to untie." ²⁸This happened in Bethany across the Jordan, where John was baptizing.

John the Baptist's Testimony to Jesus. ²⁹The next day he saw Jesus coming to-

the Baptist's role with that of Elijah, whom Malachi had prophesied would come before the day of the Lord. Here, John the Baptist will not accept either that title or that of the prophet-like-Moses whom some expected and of whom we read in the Dead Sea Scrolls. The only role he claims for himself in all four Gospels is that of the Isaian voice in the desert; his only authority for baptizing is his task to prepare the way for a greater One to follow.

23

24-27

Mk 9:11-12; Lk 1:17; Mal 4:5-6 Dt 18:15; Jn 6:14; 1QS 9, 11 Is 40:3

28   The section closes with a geographical reference that John is baptizing outside the Promised Land, on the other side of the Jordan (Bethany has not been found; other manuscripts read Bethabara, "the place of crossing over"). After the baptism, Jesus will enter the Promised Land and stay there until his people reject him, when once more he will retreat beyond the Jordan. Bethany beyond Jordan frames the public ministry of Jesus.

Jos 3:14-17

Jn 10:39-40 #4

The Baptist witnesses before the disciples—1:29-34

The next day (*Day Two*) John the Baptist presents the Lamb of God who takes away the world's sin. The Baptist may perhaps have referred only to the triumphant Lamb who in the Jewish picture of the last times was to destroy evil in the world. But the Christian reader of the Gospel would have seen other implications. Jesus is the paschal Lamb of the Christian Passover who by his death (at the very moment the paschal lambs were being killed in the Temple) delivered the world from sin, as the original paschal lamb's blood delivered the Israelites from the destroying angel. And, secondly, Jesus is the Servant of God described in Isaiah as being led without complaint like a lamb before the shearers, a man of sorrows who "bore the sins of many and made intercession for the transgressors."

30   The Baptist also tells us that Jesus existed before him—a true Johannine theme: the precreational existence of the Word.

1 Jn 3:5 Hen 90, 38; Test Jos 19, 8; Ap 5:6; 17:14 #3b 1 Pt 1:19 Jn 19:14 Ap 5:8-9; 1 Jn 2:2 Ex 12:1-13 Is 53:7-12 Acts 8:32-35; 1 Pt 2:21-25

ward him and said, "Behold, the Lamb of God, who takes away the sin of the world. ³⁰He is the one of whom I said, 'A man is coming after me who ranks ahead of me because he existed before me.' ³¹I did not know him, but the reason why I came baptizing with water was that he might be made known to Israel." ³²John testified further, saying, "I saw the Spirit come down like a dove from the sky and remain upon him. ³³I did not know him, but the one who sent me to baptize with water told me, 'On whomever you see the Spirit come down and remain, he is the one who will baptize with the holy Spirit.' ³⁴Now I have seen and testified that he is the Son of God."

The First Disciples. ³⁵The next day John was there again with two of his disciples, ³⁶and as he watched Jesus walk by, he said, "Behold, the Lamb of God." ³⁷The two disciples heard what he said and followed Jesus. ³⁸Jesus turned and saw them following him and said to them, "What are you looking for?" They said to him, "Rabbi" (which translated means Teacher), "where are you staying?" ³⁹He said to them, "Come, and you will see." So they went and saw where he was staying, and they stayed with him that day. It was about four in the afternoon. ⁴⁰Andrew, the brother of Simon Peter, was one of the two who heard John and followed Jesus. ⁴¹He first found his own

31   And as the Baptist baptized with water, Jesus will baptize with the Holy Spirit. Again Jesus' forerunner may have meant by this only the cleansing spirit of God which the Hebrew prophets spoke of as purifying people's hearts in the last days. The Dead Sea Scrolls tell us that at his visitation, "God will . . . cleanse human beings through a holy spirit from all wicked practices, and will sprinkle on them a spirit of truth as purifying water." But the evangelist intends the Christian reader to see a reference to the unique Spirit given by Jesus and Christian baptism.

Is 4:4; Ez 36:25-26; Za 12:10; 13:1 1QS 4, 20-21 #3b Acts 1:4-5

32-34   There is no mention in John of a heavenly voice at the baptism of Jesus, but the Baptist himself bears witness: Jesus is the Elect (probably better than "Son") of God upon whom the Spirit of God descended and remained—another reference to the Suffering Servant of Isaiah. Thus at the beginning of John we have a whole christology in the Baptist's witness to Jesus: the eternally existing One who is to die as the paschal lamb and Suffering Servant for the sins of men and women and then pour forth the Holy Spirit on a new Israel.

Mk 1:10-11; Lk 3:22

Is 42:1

The first disciples—1:35-51

The Synoptics have telescoped the first call of the disciples into the Galilean ministry. The fourth evangelist gives us more detail; the first disciples were disciples of John the Baptist and they were called at the Jordan river before Jesus returned to
36-40 Galilee. On a given day (*Day Three*) two disciples, Andrew and someone unnamed (the beloved disciple?), follow Jesus

Mk 1:16-20; Lk 5:1-11

brother Simon and told him, "We have found the Messiah" (which is translated Anointed). ⁴²Then he brought him to Jesus. Jesus looked at him and said, "You are Simon the son of John; you will be called Kephas" (which is translated Peter).

⁴³The next day he decided to go to Galilee, and he found Philip. And Jesus said to him, "Follow me." ⁴⁴Now Philip was from Bethsaida, the town of Andrew and Peter. ⁴⁵Philip found Nathanael and told him, "We have found the one about whom Moses wrote in the law, and also the prophets, Jesus, son of Joseph, from Nazareth." ⁴⁶But Nathanael said to him, "Can anything good come from Nazareth?" Philip said to him, "Come and see." ⁴⁷Jesus saw Nathanael coming to-

ward him and said of him, "Here is a true Israelite. There is no duplicity in him." ⁴⁸Nathanael said to him, "How do you know me?" Jesus answered and said to him, "Before Philip called you, I saw you under the fig tree." ⁴⁹Nathanael answered him, "Rabbi, you are the Son of God; you are the King of Israel." ⁵⁰Jesus answered and said to him, "Do you believe because I told you that I saw you under the fig tree? You will see greater things than this." ⁵¹And he said to him, "Amen, amen, I say to you, you will see the sky opened and the angels of God ascending and descending on the Son of Man."

2 The Wedding at Cana. ¹On the third day there was a wedding in Cana in Galilee, and the mother of Jesus was

41-42 and recognize him as Teacher. On the next day (probably, since they stayed with Jesus from 4 P.M. on: *Day Four*) Simon is brought to Jesus as to the Messiah.

43-45 On the following day (*Day Five*) Philip and Nathanael come to him and recognize him as the prophet-like-Moses, and Son of God and King of Israel (v. 49). This is obviously a technique to show the gradually increasing knowledge that the disciples gained of Jesus: from Teacher to Messiah to Son of God and King (a process that the Synoptic writers describe as going on throughout the whole public life of Jesus). Also John has telescoped here the incident of Peter's confession of Jesus as Messiah and the changing of his name, which in the Synoptics takes place later. It is one of John's tendencies to present the whole truth about Jesus in each episode.

Ps 2:6-7

Mk 1:22; 4:40; 8:29; 15:39

#8b

Mt 16:16

47 The call of Nathanael (a disciple known only to John) involves an interesting play on words. He is a true Israelite, worthy of the name of Israel (by popular etymology "a man who sees God"), and is told he shall see greater things. As the Jacob or Israel of the Old Testament saw the glory of God in **50-51** the vision of the ladder, so the Israel of the New Testament will see the glory of the Son of Man at the miracle of Cana.

Gn 28:12-17; 32:28-30

The calling of the first disciples is painted as a timelessly true portrait of vocation. The first question to be asked of one who wishes to follow is (v. 38): "What is it you seek?" Then comes the command (v. 39): "Come and see." (In John, "seeing" in the true sense means "believing"—cf. 6:40.) Those who come and believe become the new Israel: people seeing God.

Is 17:7; 30:20

there. ²Jesus and his disciples were also invited to the wedding. ³When the wine ran short, the mother of Jesus said to him, "They have no wine." ⁴[And] Jesus said to her, "Woman, how does your concern affect me? My hour has not yet come."

The wedding at Cana—2:1-11

On the third day (two days after the call of Philip: *Day Seven*), Jesus fulfills the promise of showing his new disciples his glory: his own miracle is the last of a series of witnesses to him. Galilee is the first place to behold Jesus' glory, as it will be the last, for the post-resurrection appearances of c. 21 take place in Galilee (where Nathanael and Cana are again mentioned). His mother's (John never calls her Mary) care for others is the occasion for the sign of glory.

Is 9:1-2
#4
Jn 21:2

To her observation on the lack of wine, which is not a specific request for a miracle, Jesus answers in a phrase that can only mean: "This is not my concern, but yours." And he addresses her as "woman," a polite title that is a normal address for women; but it is strange and without parallel for a son to speak thus to his mother. The reason for his refusal of common interest in Mary's request is that his "hour" has not yet come.

2 K 3:13;
Mt 8:29

Mt 15:28;
Lk 13:12;
Jn 4:21

There are many possible explanations of this enigmatic conversation; we present but one. For John the "hour" of Jesus *par excellence* is the hour of his glorification through death and resurrection. Only as this approaches can he say, "The hour has come for the Son of Man to be glorified." And when the "hour" does come, the "woman" appears again on the scene (the only two times John mentions Mary; #4). And this time her role is not rejected: she can be a caring mother, for she is given the beloved disciple, the example of the perfect Christian, as her son. Thus, by the strange use of "woman" at Cana, John seems to indicate that Jesus rejects a purely human sphere of action for Mary to reserve for her a much richer role, viz., that of a mother caring for those who would follow him.

Jn 7:30;
8:20

Jn 12:23;
13:1; 17:1
19:25-27

The title "woman" becomes more understandable in the background of Genesis. There are many references to Genesis in this first week of Jesus' activity: (a) the prologue begins with "In the beginning"—the words which are the title for Genesis in the Hebrew Bible; (b) the prologue tells of the coming of light into darkness; (c) at the baptism the Spirit descends and *remains* on Jesus just as the spirit of God moved over the face of the primeval waters; (d) the time from the baptism to Cana, the beginning of the work of the new Adam, is sometimes seen

Gn 1:1

Gn 1:2-5

Gn 1:2

28

[5]His mother said to the servers, "Do whatever he tells you." [6]Now there were six stone water jars there for Jewish ceremonial washings, each holding twenty to thirty gallons. [7]Jesus told them, "Fill the jars with water." So they filled them to the brim. [8]Then he told them, "Draw some out now and take it to the headwaiter." So they took it. [9]And when the headwaiter tasted the water that had become wine, without knowing where it came from (although the servers who had drawn the water knew), the headwaiter called the bridegroom [10]and said to him, "Everyone serves good wine first, and then when people have drunk freely, an inferior one; but you have kept the good wine until now." [11]Jesus did this as the be-

as seven days matching the seven creative days of Genesis. In this light we can compare the woman in the Garden of Eden who led Adam to the first evil act with the woman at Cana who leads the new Adam to his first glorious work. In the prophecy of Genesis we hear that God will put enmity between the woman and the serpent and that her seed will crush the serpent. In calling his mother "woman," Jesus may well be identifying her with the new Eve who will be the mother of his disciples as the old Eve was the "mother of all the living." She can play her role of intercession, however, only when her offspring on the cross has crushed the serpent. $\quad$ Gn 2:2 / Gn 3:6 / Gn 3:15 / Ap 12 / Gn 3:20 / Jn 16:11, 32-33

5 $\quad$ Nevertheless, in reply to Mary's innocent request and because of her obedient but expectant reply (for Jesus can never
6-10 resist faith), Jesus does perform a miraculous sign, i.e., a miracle which shows the onlooker something about Jesus' mission, and often shows the Christian reader something more about Jesus and the church which continues his mission. The prophets had foretold an abundance of wine in messianic days; and the abundance of wine at Cana (six jars with some twenty gallons each) would bring these prophecies to mind and point to the messianic nature of Jesus' mission. In this messianic framework the wine represents his wisdom and teaching. A further lesson for Jesus' ministry is that he replaces the Jewish purifications (v. 6) with something better. $\quad$ Mt 15:22-28 / #3b / Amos 9:13-14; Gn 27:27-28; 49:10-12 / Prv 9:4-5

In the context of the church life of the early Christians, the wine of the eucharist would come to mind, especially since John tells us that the changing of water to wine took place before Passover (v. 13), the same time that Jesus would change wine into his eucharistic blood two years later. (It is interesting too that at the cross the themes of Mary and of blood from Jesus' side [the eucharist?] come together.) In this context, Mary's statement, "They have no wine," may be a Johannine commentary on the barrenness of Judaism, as her remark, "Do whatever he tells you," is significant in the training of the ideal $\quad$ Jn 19:25, 34

ginning of his signs in Cana in Galilee and so revealed his glory, and his disciples began to believe in him.

¹²After this, he and his mother, [his] brothers, and his disciples went down to Capernaum and stayed there only a few days.

Cleansing of the Temple. ¹³Since the Passover of the Jews was near, Jesus went up to Jerusalem. ¹⁴He found in the temple area those who sold oxen, sheep, and doves, as well as the money-changers seated there. ¹⁵He made a whip out of cords and drove them all out of the temple area, with the sheep and oxen, and spilled the coins of the money-changers and overturned their tables, ¹⁶and to those who sold doves he said, "Take these out of here, and stop making my Father's house a marketplace." ¹⁷His disciples recalled the words of scripture, "Zeal for your house will consume me." ¹⁸At this

11   disciple. And we note that the result of the first sign brought about by Mary's intervention is the faith of the disciples, the completion of their vocation.

Section 2. Replacing Jewish Institutions; Reaction to Jesus

(2:13-4:54)

The cleansing of the Temple—2:13-22

In the Johannine interlocking schema, Cana is the last of the (seven?) days closing Section One, and the first of (seven?) miracles that mark Jesus' public life (4:46, official's son; c. 5, paralytic; c. 6, multiplication of loaves and walking on water; c. 9, blind man; c. 11, Lazarus). It is also the first instance of the replacement of Jewish institutions.

13   The scene shifts; Jesus goes to the capital for the first of the three Passovers that John mentions (the Synoptics telescope the public life into one year and have only one Passover). In

14   the outer court of the Temple Jesus finds a virtual market where visitors could purchase the animals necessary for sacrifice and change their money for Tyrian half-shekels (coins religiously

15-16 not objectionable). In attacking this commerce, Jesus is doing more than purging an abuse; the animals and the coins were absolutely necessary for Temple worship. In this cleansing Jesus is attacking the Temple itself. He has replaced Jewish purifications at Cana; now he shows that the very center of Jewish worship loses its meaning in his presence. The glorious presence of God, once confined to the Temple, has now become flesh in Jesus. The reference in 17 is to Ps 69:10.

The Temple authorities ("the Jews") should have understood his words: "If *you* destroy this temple, in three days I will raise it up." Jeremiah had told them that impurity would destroy

(margin references) Jn 6:4; 12:1

Mt 12:6; 27:51

1 K 9:1-3; Jn 1:14

Jer 7:11-14

30

the Jews answered and said to him, "What sign can you show us for doing this?" [19]Jesus answered and said to them, "Destroy this temple and in three days I will raise it up." [20]The Jews said, "This temple has been under construction for forty-six years, and you will raise it up in three days?" [21]But he was speaking about the temple of his body. [22]Therefore, when he was raised from the dead, his disciples remembered that he had said this, and they came to believe the scripture and the word Jesus had spoken.

[23]While he was in Jerusalem for the feast of Passover, many began to believe in his name when they saw the signs he

19 the value of the Temple in God's eyes; other Old Testament passages had told them that with the coming of the Messiah an ideal temple would appear on earth in which no commerce would be tolerated and all nations would be welcome. If "the Jews" destroyed the Temple by defiling it before God, in a short time Jesus would raise up the messianic temple.

Tob 14:5-7; Za 14:20-21

Is 56:7

20 "The Jews" understand his claim only on the material level: how can he so quickly rebuild their beautiful buildings that had taken forty-six years to construct (from 20–19 B.C. to the current A.D. 28)? In Mark/Matthew the false witnesses at the death trial of Jesus will misrepresent him as having said: "I can/will destroy the Temple." The Christian community used Jesus' words in various contexts to express the teachings of faith. As Mark points out, the temple of which he spoke is not made by hands—it is the church made of believers, says Paul.

#1 Mt 26:61 #3b

Mk 14:58

21 But John sees another message: the temple is the body of Jesus which, as the disciples would see after the resurrection, would

22 be raised up in three days (John deliberately uses "raise up," not the "construct" of the Synoptics). These two Christian interpretations of Jesus' words are in perfect harmony, for the church is the body of Christ.

1 Cor 3:16; 2 Cor 6:16; Eph 2:19-22 Ap 21:22 Col 1:24

The Synoptics place the cleansing of the Temple in the last week of Christ's life (Matthew, on Palm Sunday; Mark, on Monday), their only Passover. John may be giving us a more accurate chronology. On the other hand, he may have wished to join the Temple scene to the Baptist's introduction of Jesus, and thus show the fulfillment of Mal 3:1.

Mt 21:10-17; Mk 11:15-19

#8b

Transition—2:23-25

Some seeing Jesus' miracles accept him, but not completely; they see only the marvel of the sign, not the meaning behind

24 it. And Jesus, thoroughly knowing people (John always stresses Jesus' complete control), is not satisfied. The mention of signs done at Jerusalem (of which we know nothing) may be meant to include the cleansing of the Temple or may be a vague gener-

was doing. ²⁴But Jesus would not trust himself to them because he knew them all, ²⁵and did not need anyone to testify about human nature. He himself understood it well.

3 **Nicodemus.** ¹Now there was a Pharisee named Nicodemus, a ruler of the Jews. ²He came to Jesus at night and said to him, "Rabbi, we know that you are a teacher who has come from God, for no one can do these signs that you are doing unless God is with him." ³Jesus answered and said to him, "Amen, amen, I say to you, no one can see the kingdom of God without being born from above." ⁴Nicodemus said to him, "How can a person once grown old be born again? Surely he cannot reenter his mother's womb and be born again, can he?" ⁵Jesus answered, "Amen, amen, I say to you, no one can

alization giving a setting for the inadequacy of Nicodemus' belief. See 21:25.

Nicodemus—3:1-21

Ancient Jewish literature tells us that God showed his approval of a certain rabbi's teaching by working miracles through him. To Nicodemus, a member of the Sanhedrin or governing body ("ruler"), Jesus' marvels mean exactly that; and so he comes to Jesus out of the night (in John, darkness is symbolic of evil and ignorance) and salutes him as a great teacher. The first disciples had also recognized Jesus as a teacher but soon progressed beyond that, as the succeeding titles in chapter one tell us. Here too Jesus will show Nicodemus that he is a "teacher from God" in a way Nicodemus does not expect: he has *actually* come from God.

Jesus begins by stating that, since God is above, the only way one can enter his kingdom is to be born or begotten from above. The whole discourse will stress that what is on the natural level, the level of flesh, cannot reach the divine level without being boosted up. And that lifting up is accomplished by God descending from heaven to the human level, and then returning again to heaven, drawing human beings up with him—the whole Johannine theology of the incarnation, redemptive death, resurrection, and ascension.

The key word in the discourse is in v. 3: "without being born *anōthen*"; the Greek *anōthen* has the double meaning of "from above" and "again." Nicodemus, thinking on a purely human level, takes the meaning "again," which leads to an impossibility. In an effort to explain, Jesus then speaks of being born or begotten of water and the spirit. Nicodemus should have understood this, for he knows that the spirit or breath given by God is responsible for natural life, and that in messianic times God would sprinkle clean water on people and give

Jn 13:30

Jn 1:38

#2

#3a
#1

DBS 1615

Gn 2:7;
Jb 34:14
Ez
36:25-26;

3

4

5

enter the kingdom of God without being born of water and Spirit. ⁶What is born of flesh is flesh and what is born of spirit is spirit. ⁷Do not be amazed that I told you, 'You must be born from above.' ⁸ The wind blows where it wills, and you can hear the sound it makes, but you do not know where it comes from or where it goes; so it is with everyone who is born of the Spirit." ⁹Nicodemus answered and said to him, "How can this happen?" ¹⁰Jesus answered and said to him, "You are the teacher of Israel and you do not understand this? ¹¹Amen, amen, I say to you, we speak of what we know and we testify to what we have seen, but you people do not accept our testimony. ¹²If I tell you about earthly things and you do not believe, how will you believe if I tell you about heavenly things? ¹³No one has gone up to heaven except the one who has come down from heaven, the Son of Man. ¹⁴And just as Moses lifted up the serpent in the desert, so must the Son of Man be lifted up, ¹⁵so that everyone who believes in him may have eternal life."

¹⁶For God so loved the world that he gave his only Son, so that everyone who

	them a new spirit, i.e., a new form of life. (The Christian reader would have an extended understanding of the passage and see	Jn 1:31
7-8	it in the light of baptism and the Holy Spirit.) When Nicodemus still does not understand, Jesus gives him an example. One	#3b; Jn 7:38-39
	believes in the wind without understanding its workings; he must do likewise with the spirit (the same Hebrew word—likewise in Greek—means "wind" and "spirit").	#3a
9-10	When Nicodemus still presses, Jesus reminds him that he, Nicodemus, is supposed to be the teacher, not the pupil. He had come as a representative of "the Jews" saying, "We know" (v. 2—are the "we" other members of the Sanhedrin?). He	Jn 12:42
11	must now listen as Jesus speaks for the Christians, "We speak of what we know," but "the Jews" whom he represents will not accept this witness. Yet, if Nicodemus really wants to	
12	understand, Jesus will explain further. Although, frankly, if he cannot understand the things he should have known ("earthly"), how can he hope to understand when Jesus reaches	
13-14	up to heaven? This is the first of John's three Son-of-Man-being-lifted-up sayings, comparable to Mark's three Son of Man passion sayings. By twofold meaning the word "lift up" refers both	Mk 8:31; 9:31; 10:33
	to being lifted up on the cross and being lifted up into heaven. In Jesus' return to his Father in heaven, the cross is the first	#3a
	step on the ladder of the ascension. Only when Jesus is raised up can the Spirit of which he has spoken to Nicodemus be	Jn 7:39
	given. (Moses' serpent is an example of salvation coming through raising up on a cross.)	Nm 21:9; Wis 16:5-7
16	The dialogue has now become a monologue (Nicodemus seems to slip off into the night whence he came) in which the	#6
	import of the incarnation is developed. God gave (in incarnation but perhaps also in death) his only Son to gain this new	Rom 8:32; Gal 2:20

believes in him might not perish but might have eternal life. [17]For God did not send his Son into the world to condemn the world, but that the world might be saved through him. [18]Whoever believes in him will not be condemned, but whoever does not believe has already been condemned, because he has not believed in the name of the only Son of God. [19]And this is the verdict, that the light came into the world, but people preferred darkness to light, because their works were evil. [20]For everyone who does wicked things hates the light and does not come toward the light, so that his works might not be exposed. [21]But whoever lives the truth comes to the light, so that his works may be clearly seen as done in God.

Final Witness of the Baptist. [22]After this, Jesus and his disciples went into the region of Judea, where he spent some time with them baptizing. [23]John was also baptizing in Aenon near Salim, because there was an abundance of water there, and people came to be baptized, [24]for John had not yet been imprisoned. [25]Now a dispute arose between the disciples of John and a Jew about ceremonial washings. [26]So they came to John and said to him, "Rabbi, the one who was with you across the Jordan, to whom you testified, here he is baptizing and everyone is coming to

17
18
life for us. Therefore, the mission of Jesus is not for condemnation (the same Greek word means "condemnation" and "judgment") but salvation. Nevertheless, the very presence of Jesus constitutes a judgment—realized eschatology. #3a #5

19-21
Evil is darkness; with Jesus, the light has come into the darkness. But the darkness will not receive it, and this very refusal constitutes judgment (theology, too, tells us that in condemning to hell God is simply accepting people's state of will at their death; they have turned away from God and God leaves them to their fate). In this picture of a world divided into light and darkness, there are interesting parallels between the Dead Sea Scrolls and the Fourth Gospel. Concluding this section, we should notice that Jesus, in stressing the necessity of spiritual rebirth, has negated the importance of natural birth into the Chosen People; another pillar of Judaism has been replaced. Jn 1:5 1QS 3, 18-21; 4, 23-24

The Baptist's last witness—3:22-30

Without much transition the narrative returns to John the Baptist. There is no exact sequence between verses 21-22. Jerusalem is in Judea; one can scarcely leave Jerusalem and come into the region of Judea. Aenon near Salim has not been identified with certainty; it is either in the upper Jordan valley or, more probably, in Samaria near Shechem. The time indication is interesting since it places all of Jesus' ministry in cc. 1–3 before the Baptist's arrest. The Synoptics know only of a ministry after that event. The success of Jesus puzzles the precursor's followers and their complaint gives the Baptist a final chance to bear witness.

23
24
Mk 1:14

25-26
Mt 11:2-3

him." ²⁷John answered and said, "No one can receive anything except what has been given him from heaven. ²⁸You yourselves can testify that I said [that] I am not the Messiah, but that I was sent before him. ²⁹The one who has the bride is the bridegroom; the best man, who stands and listens for him, rejoices greatly at the bridegroom's voice. So this joy of mine has been made complete. ³⁰He must increase; I must decrease."

The One from Heaven. ³¹The one who comes from above is above all. The one who is of the earth is earthly and speaks of earthly things. But the one who comes from heaven [is above all]. ³²He testifies to what he has seen and heard, but no one accepts his testimony. ³³Whoever does accept his testimony certifies that God is trustworthy. ³⁴ For the one whom God sent speaks the words of God. He does not ration his gift of the Spirit. ³⁵The Father loves the Son and has given everything over to him. ³⁶Whoever believes in the Son has eternal life, but whoever disobeys the Son will not see life, but the wrath of God remains upon him.

4 ¹Now when Jesus learned that the Pharisees had heard that Jesus was making and baptizing more disciples than John ²(although Jesus himself was not baptizing, just his disciples), ³he left Judea and returned to Galilee.

The Samaritan Woman. ⁴He had to

27-30 He does so in terms of the famous Old Testament symbol of Israel as the bride of God. The true Israel has been solemnly betrothed to God, and now Jesus is coming to claim his bride. In Jewish weddings the bridegroom came with his friends to the bride's house to take her to his home. His best friend had been standing guard at the bride's house to make sure that no one entered before he came. As the friend, the Baptist hears the bridegroom coming to claim Israel his bride, and rejoices that he can withdraw into the background.

Ex 34:14; Hos 2:19; Is 54:6

2 Cor 11:2; Ap 19:7; 21:2

Echoes from the discourse with Nicodemus—3:31-36

#7

This speech seems to be a duplicate of the speech to Nicodemus in the earlier part of the chapter and almost every verse has a counterpart there. These verses, then, are to be understood in the light of Nicodemus' problem; they resemble Jesus' revelation even if, in context, they seem to be the Baptist's words.

v. 31 = 6, 13
32 = 11
33-36 = 15-18

Return to Galilee—4:1-4

The reference to Jesus' baptizing supplies the motive for the return from Judea to Galilee through Samaria. The parenthetic, 2 editorial remark that Jesus himself did not baptize seems designed to clarify (or correct) 3:22 and 4:1. Perhaps the Johannine redactor considered baptism by Jesus' disciples not to be baptism with the Holy Spirit (for the Spirit would not be given until Jesus had returned to his Father) but a continuation of the Baptist's work.

Jn 7:39; Acts 1:5

pass through Samaria. ⁵So he came to a town of Samaria called Sychar, near the plot of land that Jacob had given to his son Joseph. ⁶Jacob's well was there. Jesus, tired from his journey, sat down there at the well. It was about noon.

⁷A woman of Samaria came to draw water. Jesus said to her, "Give me a drink." ⁸His disciples had gone into the town to buy food. ⁹The Samaritan woman said to him, "How can you, a Jew, ask me, a Samaritan woman, for a drink?" (For Jews use nothing in common with Samaritans.) ¹⁰Jesus answered and said to her, "If you knew the gift of God and who is saying to you, 'Give me a drink,' you would have asked him and he would have given you living water." ¹¹[The woman] said to him, "Sir, you do not even have a bucket and the cistern is deep; where then can you get this living water? ¹²Are you greater than our father Jacob, who gave us this cistern and drank from it himself with his children and his flocks?" ¹³Jesus answered and said to her, "Everyone who drinks this water will be

Discourse with the Samaritan woman—4:4-42

The Samaritan town is probably Shechem (misspelled "Sychar"; the Syriac has "Shechem"), a famous Old Testament locale connected with the Jacob stories. Traditionally the Samaritans were the descendants of intermarriage between the Israelites of the Northern Kingdom and pagan colonists whom the Assyrian conquerors had settled in the land. Their religion was basically Mosaic but with pagan admixtures. They accepted only the first five books of the Old Testament, rejecting the prophets and all the prophetic emphasis on the Jerusalem Temple. This caused great hostility between them and the Jews, and about a hundred years before Christ the Jewish high priest had destroyed the Samaritan temple on Mount Gerizim. The Synoptics have left no record of any ministry of Jesus among the Samaritans; yet the early Christian church quickly evangelized Samaria.

Gn 33:18ff

2 K 17:24-34

Neh 4:1ff; Sir 50:25-26

Mt 10:5; Lk 9:51-56 Acts 1:8; 8:1-25

6-8 With this background, we can well imagine the amazement of the Samaritan woman at this Jewish man who asks her for a favor. The conversation that ensues follows the typical instruction pattern of Johannine misunderstanding. "Living" or running water, spring water, is greatly prized in Palestine, where, otherwise, during the long rainless months one must depend on cisterns which have stored up the previous winter's rains. In literature this precious water became a symbol of divine wisdom and teaching. The Samaritan woman understands only natural water, but Jesus is referring to his divine revelation and to the Holy Spirit who will be given as living water to those who accept that revelation. The Christian community would probably have understood it in a sacramental context, viz., the water of baptism which initiates into Jesus' teaching and confers the Holy Spirit.

10 *#1*

11 *Is 55:1-3; Ps 36:9; Jer 2:13*

Jn 7:38-39

#3b

36

thirsty again; [14]but whoever drinks the water I shall give will never thirst; the water I shall give will become in him a spring of water welling up to eternal life." [15]The woman said to him, "Sir, give me this water, so that I may not be thirsty or have to keep coming here to draw water."

[16]Jesus said to her, "Go call your husband and come back." [17]The woman answered and said to him, "I do not have a husband." Jesus answered her, "You are right in saying, 'I do not have a husband.' [18]For you have had five husbands, and the one you have now is not your husband. What you have said is true." [19]The woman said to him, "Sir, I can see that you are a prophet. [20]Our ancestors worshiped on this mountain; but you people say that the place to worship is in Jerusalem." [21]Jesus said to her, "Believe me, woman, the hour is coming when you will worship the Father neither on this mountain nor in Jerusalem. [22]You people

worship what you do not understand; we worship what we understand, because salvation is from the Jews. [23]But the hour is coming, and is now here, when true worshipers will worship the Father in Spirit and truth; and indeed the Father seeks such people to worship him. [24]God is Spirit, and those who worship him must worship in Spirit and truth." [25]The woman said to him, "I know that the Messiah is coming, the one called the Anointed; when he comes, he will tell us everything." [26]Jesus said to her, "I am he, the one who is speaking with you."

[27]At that moment his disciples returned, and were amazed that he was talking with a woman, but still no one said, "What are you looking for?" or "Why are you talking with her?" [28]The woman left her water jar and went into the town and said to the people, [29]"Come see a man who told me everything I have done. Could he possibly be the Messiah?" [30]They went out of the town and came to

12 She asks, can Jesus possibly be greater than Jacob who 13-14 found this well? Jesus' answer supplies us with a magnificent description of baptism: "A spring of water welling up to eternal life." When the woman still misunderstands, Jesus gives 15 16-18 her a sign: his superhuman knowledge of her past. Impressed, 19-20 the woman recognizes a prophet (like the lawgiver Moses) and so presents him a legal question on the place of worship. 21-22 While Jesus defends the purity of the Jewish tradition as opposed to the heretical Samaritans ("Jews" here, by exception, is not opprobrious; Jesus is speaking with a foreigner), he offers both nations a place in the worship of his 23 new Israel, a worship not dependent on locality, but flowing from the Spirit of Truth ("spirit" and "truth" are a hendiadys) 24 which he will confer. God gives the Spirit. (We find three great equations in the Fourth Gospel and First John: "God is spirit"; "God is light"; "God is love." These are not definitions of God's essence, but refer to God's relation to people. He gives them the Spirit; he loves them; he gives them his Son, their light.) And the Spirit enables them to worship the Father. 25-26 This statement finally leads the woman to realize that perhaps the Messiah stands before her. Leaving the jar—no longer 28-30 useful for this type of living water—the Samaritan hastens to

#2

Jn 1:48-50
Cf. 1:21

1 Jn 1:5;
4:8
Jn
14:16-17;
3:16; 1:4

him. ³¹Meanwhile, the disciples urged him, "Rabbi, eat." ³²But he said to them, "I have food to eat of which you do not know." ³³So the disciples said to one another, "Could someone have brought him something to eat?" ³⁴Jesus said to them, "My food is to do the will of the one who sent me and to finish his work. ³⁵Do you not say, 'In four months the harvest will be here'? I tell you, look up and see the fields ripe for the harvest. ³⁶The reaper is already receiving his payment and gathering crops for eternal life, so that the sower and reaper can rejoice together. ³⁷For here the saying is verified that 'One sows and another reaps.' ³⁸I sent you to reap what you have not worked for;

others have done the work, and you are sharing the fruits of their work."

³⁹Many of the Samaritans of that town began to believe in him because of the word of the woman who testified, "He told me everything I have done." ⁴⁰When the Samaritans came to him, they invited him to stay with them; and he stayed there two days. ⁴¹Many more began to believe in him because of his word, ⁴²and they said to the woman, "We no longer believe because of your word; for we have heard for ourselves, and we know that this is truly the savior of the world."

Return to Galilee. ⁴³After the two days, he left there for Galilee. ⁴⁴For Jesus himself testified that a prophet has no

41-42 lead others to Jesus. When many of her kinsmen do believe in Jesus, she finds that, like the Baptist, she decreases when Jesus increases (verses 41-42). By evangelizing them, she comes to full faith.

27,31   Meanwhile the disciples return from their shopping and
32-34 offer food to their Master. But his food is of a higher order: the work of his Father, namely salvation. And he has already eaten, for he sees salvation coming to the Samaritans. Look-
35-36 ing over the fertile plain near Shechem, already ripe for the harvest, he cites a proverb. (If the "harvest" is a time indication, we may be in May–June, after the Passover of March–April in 2:23.) In the natural order, the proverb says, four months elapse between planting and harvest; but in the supernatural order, faith ripens quickly and the sower and reaper
37-38 can rejoice together. The disciples too must learn to harvest the crop of believers even though they have not sowed the seed. In Acts 8:4-25 Philip the Hellenist evangelizes Samaria, and then the Jerusalem apostles send Peter and John to confirm the conversion.

Is 55:1-3;
Sir 24:18;
Jn 17:2-4;
Heb 10:7

Jesus heals the son of a royal official—4:43-54

After two days Jesus proceeds again to Cana of Galilee. (Is it a coincidence that both Cana miracles take place on the third day, and both test the faith of the petitioner?) The reference
44 to the lack of honor in Galilee ("his native place"?) echoes the Synoptic tradition that when Jesus returned to Galilee, he was not received.

Jn 2:1

Lk 4:14-30

honor in his native place. [45]When he came into Galilee, the Galileans welcomed him, since they had seen all he had done in Jerusalem at the feast; for they themselves had gone to the feast.

Second Sign at Cana. [46]Then he returned to Cana in Galilee, where he had made the water wine. Now there was a royal official whose son was ill in Capernaum. [47]When he heard that Jesus had arrived in Galilee from Judea, he went to him and asked him to come down and heal his son, who was near death. [48]Jesus said to him, "Unless you people see signs and wonders, you will not believe." [49]The royal official said to him, "Sir, come down before my child dies." [50]Jesus said to him, "You may go; your son will live." The man believed what Jesus said to him and left. [51]While he was on his way back, his slaves met him and told him that his boy would live. [52]He asked them when he began to recover. They told him, "The fever left him yesterday, about one in the afternoon." [53]The father realized that just at that time Jesus had said to him, "Your son will live," and he and his whole household came to believe. [54][Now] this was the second sign Jesus did when he came to Galilee from Judea.

5 Cure on a Sabbath. [1]After this, there was a feast of the Jews, and Jesus

46-53   The story of the royal official's son is probably a third variant of the story of the centurion's boy, which already has two slightly different forms in Matthew and Luke (the variants touch inconsequential details and are of a sort that could arise in oral tradition). Because the Synoptic centurion is a pagan, some would construct a development of faith in John from the *Jew* Nicodemus through the *half-Jew, half-pagan* Samaritan to the *pagan* official. But John never indicates that the official is pagan. The story is self-explanatory, but notice the emphasis on *life* (verses 50, 51, 53). To Nicodemus, Jesus had spoken of a rebirth to a new life; to the Samaritan, of living water springing up to eternal life; here we have the climax of restored life.

Mt 8:5-13; Lk 7:1-10

Lk 7:4-5

Section 3. Replacing Feasts of "the Jews" (5:1–10:42)

Section Two began after the first Cana miracle and ended with the second Cana miracle. Jesus has shown that he is to replace the Jewish purifications and Temple. Now he replaces the great feasts one by one. We also see a continuation of the "life" theme that reaches a climax in the bread of life in chapter six.

#4

At the pool of Bethesda—5:1-9

It is not clear which feast is referred to in 5:1; some have thought of Pentecost (fifty days after Passover), the feast of the spring harvest. Eventually (by this time?) Pentecost became the feast of renewing the Sinai covenant since Moses arrived

Cf. Jn 4:35; Lv 23:15-22 Ex 19:1

went up to Jerusalem. ²Now there is in Jerusalem at the Sheep [Gate] a pool called in Hebrew Bethesda, with five porticoes. ³In these lay a large number of ill, blind, lame, and crippled. [⁴] ⁵One man was there who had been ill for thirty-eight years. ⁶When Jesus saw him lying there and knew that he had been ill for a long time, he said to him, "Do you want to be well?" ⁷The sick man answered him, "Sir, I have no one to put me into the pool when the water is stirred up; while I am on my way, someone else gets down there before me." ⁸Jesus said to him, "Rise, take up your mat, and walk." ⁹Immediately the man became well, took up his mat, and walked.

Now that day was a sabbath. ¹⁰So the Jews said to the man who was cured, "It is the sabbath, and it is not lawful for you to carry your mat." ¹¹He answered them, "The man who made me well told me, 'Take up your mat and walk.'" ¹²They asked him, "Who is the man who told you, 'Take it up and walk'?" ¹³The man who was healed did not know who it was, for Jesus had slipped away, since there was a crowd there. ¹⁴After this Jesus found him in the temple area and said to him, "Look, you are well; do not sin any more, so that nothing worse may happen to you." ¹⁵The man went and told the Jews that Jesus was the one who had made him well. ¹⁶Therefore, the Jews began to persecute Jesus because he did this on a sabbath. ¹⁷But Jesus answered them, "My Father is at work until now, so I am at work." ¹⁸For this reason the Jews tried

at Sinai roughly fifty days after the Passover in Egypt. The references to Jesus the judge (vss. 22, 30) and to Moses' witness to Jesus (46-47) then would echo Sinai law and covenant themes associated with the feast of Pentecost. However, John emphasizes only the Sabbath feast to which we confine our remarks.

2   Light has been thrown upon the scene at Bethesda by the recent archaeological discovery of a large pool not far from the gate through which sheep were brought to the Temple. The mss. of John give different forms of the name of the pool: Bethsaida, Bezatha, Bethesda. The last is closest to the name of this pool with twin basins, now known from the Qumran Copper

3-4 Scroll: *Bet 'Eshdâ*, "House of Flowing." Evidently there was a tradition that when new water bubbled up in the pool, it had special curative effects. (Verses 3b-4, concerning an angel stirring the water, are missing from the best manuscripts and

5-8 reflect popular tradition.) In the healing there is no prerequisite of faith. This miracle has another purpose: to clarify Jesus' work.

A problem regarding Sabbath observances—5:10-18

Later there existed a specific rabbinic prohibition against carrying one's bed on a Sabbath. In ordering the man to take his mat, Jesus gives the authorities ("Jews") an excuse to question

17   why he *works* on the Sabbath. Jesus does not justify his action on humanitarian grounds, as often in the Synoptics, but

Lk 13:15;
14:5
Mt 12:5-8

all the more to kill him, because he not only broke the sabbath but he also called God his own father, making himself equal to God.

The Work of the Son. [19]Jesus answered and said to them, "Amen, amen, I say to you, a son cannot do anything on his own, but only what he sees his father doing; for what he does, his son will do also. [20]For the Father loves his Son and shows him everything that he himself does, and he will show him greater works than these, so that you may be amazed. [21]For just as the Father raises the dead and gives life, so also does the Son give life to whomever he wishes. [22]Nor does the Father judge anyone, but he has given all judgment to his Son, [23]so that all may honor the Son just as they honor the Father. Whoever does not honor the Son does not honor the Father who sent him.

[24]Amen, amen, I say to you, whoever hears my word and believes in the one who sent me has eternal life and will not come to condemnation, but has passed from death to life. [25]Amen, amen, I say to you, the hour is coming and is now here when the dead will hear the voice of the Son of God, and those who hear will live. [26]For just as the Father has life in himself, so also he gave to his Son the possession of life in himself. [27]And he gave him power to exercise judgment, because he is the Son of Man. [28]Do not be amazed at this, because the hour is coming in which all who are in the tombs will hear his voice [29]and will come out, those who have done good deeds to the resurrection of life, but those who have done wicked deeds to the resurrection of condemnation.

[30]"I cannot do anything on my own; I

---

on grounds that reveal his supreme authority. Despite the biblical statement that God rested from creative activity on the Sabbath, the later rabbis realized that God could not have ceased his providential maintenance of the universe on the Sabbath. Thus they admitted that God continued to work on the Sabbath in giving life and rewarding good and punishing evil. Jesus' answer may refer to this belief. The clear implication that he is equal to God is not lost on "the Jews," who accuse him of appropriating divine power to himself.

Gn 2:3

The work of Jesus—5:19-30

Jesus replies that he is appropriating nothing to himself, for he does only what he sees the Father doing. And the very

21-23 works "the Jews" admit that God does on the Sabbath—giving life, judging—are those that the Father has entrusted to him.

24-25 Only belief in his mission will confer spiritual life and deliver from the death of sin. (Note that judgment and the gift of life are present realities—another instance of realized eschatology.)

26-30 Verses 26-30 seem to be a variant form of the speech of 19-25, with the emphasis on future judgment and life given on the last day (parousia eschatology). Both eschatological views become part of later Christian theology, for the life of grace we receive on earth is the beginning of the life of beatific vision to be possessed in heaven.

#5

#7

v. 26 = 21
27 = 22
28:28 =
20b, 25
30 = 19

judge as I hear, and my judgment is just, because I do not seek my own will but the will of the one who sent me.

Witnesses to Jesus. [31]"If I testify on my own behalf, my testimony cannot be verified. [32]But there is another who testifies on my behalf, and I know that the testimony he gives on my behalf is true. [33]You sent emissaries to John, and he testified to the truth. [34]I do not accept testimony from a human being, but I say this so that you may be saved. [35]He was a burning and shining lamp, and for a while you were content to rejoice in his light. [36]But I have testimony greater than John's. The works that the Father gave me to accomplish, these works that I perform testify on my behalf that the Father has sent me. [37]Moreover, the Father who sent me has testified on my behalf. But you have never heard his voice nor seen his form, [38]and you do not have his word remaining in you, because you do not believe in the one whom he has sent. [39]You search

the scriptures, because you think you have eternal life through them; even they testify on my behalf. [40]But you do not want to come to me to have life.

Unbelief of Jesus' Hearers. [41]"I do not accept human praise; [42]moreover, I know that you do not have the love of God in you. [43]I came in the name of my Father, but you do not accept me; yet if another comes in his own name, you will accept him. [44]How can you believe, when you accept praise from one another and do not seek the praise that comes from the only God? [45]Do not think that I will accuse you before the Father: the one who will accuse you is Moses, in whom you have placed your hope. [46]For if you had believed Moses, you would have believed me, because he wrote about me. [47]But if you do not believe his writings, how will you believe my words?"

6 **Multiplication of the Loaves.** [1]After this, Jesus went across the Sea of Galilee [of Tiberias]. [2]A large crowd followed

Witnesses for Jesus' claims—5:31-47

Jesus has presented his claims; he now calls on his witnesses.

33-35 First, the Baptist; he was a lamp like Elijah, but not the light. Despite the enthusiasm he aroused, "the Jews" remain unwilling

36 to accept his witness to Jesus. Second, Jesus' own works bear

37 witness to him, as Nicodemus admitted. Third, if they will accept it, the Father is his witness, having prepared the way for him in the Old Testament. At Sinai only Moses dealt directly with God, and the people were obliged to accept his word.

38 Now they will not accept the one whom God has sent. Finally,

39 the Scriptures bear witness to Jesus. (Notice the life theme.)

40-43 Yet, Jesus knows the Pharisees: they will not accept these

44 witnesses. Here John exacerbates the Synoptic tradition against the Jewish authorities: they have no love of God, only a

45-47 desire for human praise. As a result, their own Moses will accuse them; for here stands the prophet-like-Moses, and they do not heed him as Moses commanded.

Sir 48:1; Jn 1:8

Jn 3:2; 7:31

Mt 23

Dt 18:15

The multiplication of the loaves—6:1-15

After an undefinable temporal gap, John picks up the story in Galilee the following spring, near the second Passover. The

Cf. 2:13

him, because they saw the signs he was performing on the sick. ³Jesus went up on the mountain, and there he sat down with his disciples. ⁴The Jewish feast of Passover was near. ⁵When Jesus raised his eyes and saw that a large crowd was coming to him, he said to Philip, "Where can we buy enough food for them to eat?" ⁶He said this to test him, because he himself knew what he was going to do. ⁷Philip answered him, "Two hundred days' wages worth of food would not be enough for each of them to have a little [bit]." ⁸One of his disciples, Andrew, the brother of Simon Peter, said to him, ⁹"There is a boy here who has five barley loaves and two fish; but what good are these for so many?" ¹⁰Jesus said, "Have the people recline." Now there was a great deal of grass in that place. So the men reclined, about five thousand in number. ¹¹Then Jesus took the loaves, gave thanks, and distrib-

multiplication of the loaves and fishes is narrated in all four Gospels in substantially the same form with only minor variants of place and circumstance. (The reader should compare Mark and John carefully.) Luke and John have only one multiplication narrative; Matthew and Mark have two. Interestingly, the sequence of events in John resembles closely that in Mark without Mark's second multiplication: Lk 9:10ff Mk 6:30ff; 8:1-10

Multiplication for 5000	Jn 6:1-15	Mk 6:30-44
Walking on the sea	16-24	45-54
(then skipping to after Mark's second multiplication—Mk 8:1-10)		
Request for a sign	25-34	8:11-13
Discourse on bread	35-58	14-21
Faith of Peter	59-69	27-30
Passion theme, denial	70-71	31-33

5-8 In John there is no teaching before the multiplication of the loaves. Jesus is seated on a mountain (reminiscent of Sinai?) waiting for the people and brings up the question of providing food for them himself. The introduction of Philip and Andrew as characters in the scene is typical of John. Only John mentions a young boy (or "servant") and *barley* loaves, details reminiscent of Elisha's miracle. The story of the multiplication in the Fourth Gospel has several proper details intended to remind the Christian reader of the eucharist (to which the narrative returns in verses 51-58). John alone: (a) uses the verb *eucharisteō*, "to give thanks," from which we derive "eucharist"; (b) has Jesus himself distribute the bread as he will at the Last Supper; (c) has Jesus *command* the disciples to gather up the fragments lest they perish (the Greek "to gather up" is *synagō*, whence our "synaxis," the first part of the Mass. The Greek word for "fragments," *klasma*, appears in early Christian literature as a technical name for the host.)

Mk 6:34

9
11-12

Jn 1:40, 43-44; 12:22 2 K 4:42-44

Mk 6:41; 14:22

uted them to those who were reclining, and also as much of the fish as they wanted. ¹²When they had had their fill, he said to his disciples, "Gather the fragments left over, so that nothing will be wasted." ¹³So they collected them, and filled twelve wicker baskets with fragments from the five barley loaves that had been more than they could eat. ¹⁴When the people saw the sign he had done, they said, "This is truly the Prophet, the one who is to come into the world." ¹⁵Since Jesus knew that they were going to come and carry him off to make him king, he withdrew again to the mountain alone.

Walking on the Water. ¹⁶When it was evening, his disciples went down to the sea, ¹⁷embarked in a boat, and went across the sea to Capernaum. It had already grown dark, and Jesus had not yet come to them. ¹⁸The sea was stirred up because a strong wind was blowing. ¹⁹When they had rowed about three or four miles, they saw Jesus walking on the sea and coming near the boat, and they began to be afraid. ²⁰But he said to them, "It is I. Do not be afraid." ²¹They wanted to take him into the boat, but the boat immediately arrived at the shore to which they were heading.

The Bread of Life Discourse. ²²The next day, the crowd that remained across the sea saw that there had been only one boat there, and that Jesus had not gone along with his disciples in the boat, but only his disciples had left. ²³Other boats came from Tiberias near the place where they had eaten the bread when the Lord gave thanks. ²⁴When the crowd saw that neither Jesus nor his disciples were there, they themselves got into boats and came to Capernaum looking for Jesus. ²⁵And when they found him across the sea they said to him, "Rabbi, when did you get here?" ²⁶Jesus answered them and said, "Amen, amen, I say to you, you are looking for me not because you saw signs but because you ate the loaves and were

14-15 In Mark, Jesus forces his disciples to leave immediately; John alone gives us the reason, viz., the people wanted to make him their earthly king (note how Jesus is tempted in cc. 6–7). [Mk 6:45; Third temptation; Mt 4:8-9]

Jesus walks on the Sea of Galilee—6:16-24

20 As in Mark and Matthew, the disciples are well out at sea in the midst of a storm when Jesus comes to them across the water. But the point of the story in John is not any calming of the sea, but the majestic statement: "Do not be afraid. I AM!" This "I am" may be seen as a form of the divine name revealed at Sinai to Moses before the first Passover. (Some scholars even see the theme of the crossing of the Red Sea in the walking on the water.) [Is 43:10, 25; 52:6; Ex 3:14; Ex c. 14]

Request for a sign—6:25-34

25 The crowd follows him to Capernaum and asks him, "How did you come here?" By Johannine play on words, Jesus will tell them he came here from heaven. (Notice how closely the subsequent conversation resembles that in c. 4). As always their aspirations are on the material level: they see the miraculous 27-30 element of the sign but not its meaning. Jesus tries to raise them [V. 27 = 4:13; 30-31 = 4:12; 33 = 4:14; 34 = 4:15]

filled. [27]Do not work for food that perishes but for the food that endures for eternal life, which the Son of Man will give you. For on him the Father, God, has set his seal." [28]So they said to him, "What can we do to accomplish the works of God?" [29]Jesus answered and said to them, "This is the work of God, that you believe in the one he sent." [30]So they said to him, "What sign can you do, that we may see and believe in you? What can you do? [31]Our ancestors ate manna in the desert, as it is written:

'He gave them bread from heaven to eat.'"
[32]So Jesus said to them, "Amen, amen, I say to you, it was not Moses who gave the bread from heaven; my Father gives you the true bread from heaven. [33]For the bread of God is that which comes down from heaven and gives life to the world."
[34]So they said to him, "Sir, give us this bread always." [35]Jesus said to them, "I am the bread of life; whoever comes to me will never hunger, and whoever believes in me will never thirst. [36]But I told you

31   above their materialistic outlook but is met with a persistent inability to understand. "The Jews" themselves introduce the Passover theme of the manna of the exodus. (Rabbinic literature expected the Messiah to repeat the miracle of the manna.)

32-33   But these Galileans do not recognize that the messianic manna is the word of God, divine teaching and wisdom (Dt 8:3; Prv 9:2-5). It is not the bread of the desert given by Moses but Jesus the bread given now by the Father.

(margin notes: #1 First temptation; Mt 4:3-4; Ex 16; Wis 16:20)

Discourse on the Bread of Life—6:35-58

In response to their request for bread, Jesus begins his great discourse on the bread of life. There are two parts. In the first (verses 35-50) the nourishing heavenly bread is the revelation or teaching of Jesus (sapiential theme); in the second (verses 51-58) it is the eucharist (sacramental theme). The great exegete, Fr. Lagrange, held that verses 51-58 with their sublime sacramental theology could not possibly have been understood by an unprepared Galilean audience if they were historically spoken on this occasion. If the sapiential theme was the first topic of the reflective discourse, then to bring out the deeper sacramental meaning of heavenly bread (which could be seen only after the institution of the eucharist) the Johannine redactor has combined the bread of heaven with eucharistic material from the Last Supper and so formed the second part of the speech as a parallel to the first. This accounts for John's omission of the institution of the eucharist at the Last Supper; its substance has been moved here. The two themes, sapiential and sacramental, are complementary: the proclaimed word and the Word in the sacrament have constituted the basic substance of Christian liturgy ever since.

(margin notes: #3b; #7; #8a)

that although you have seen [me], you do not believe. ³⁷Everything that the Father gives me will come to me, and I will not reject anyone who comes to me, ³⁸because I came down from heaven not to do my own will but the will of the one who sent me. ³⁹And this is the will of the one who sent me, that I should not lose anything of what he gave me, but that I should raise it [on] the last day. ⁴⁰For this is the will of my Father, that everyone who sees the Son and believes in him may have eternal life, and I shall raise him [on] the last day."

⁴¹The Jews murmured about him because he said, "I am the bread that came down from heaven," ⁴²and they said, "Is this not Jesus, the son of Joseph? Do we not know his father and mother? Then how can he say, 'I have come down from heaven'?" ⁴³Jesus answered and said to them, "Stop murmuring among yourselves. ⁴⁴No one can come to me unless the Father who sent me draw him, and I will raise him on the last day. ⁴⁵It is written in the prophets:

'They shall all be taught by God.'

Everyone who listens to my Father and learns from him comes to me. ⁴⁶Not that anyone has seen the Father except the one who is from God; he has seen the Father. ⁴⁷Amen, amen, I say to you, whoever believes has eternal life. ⁴⁸I am the bread of life. ⁴⁹Your ancestors ate the manna in the desert, but they died; ⁵⁰this is the bread that comes down from heaven so that one may eat it and not die. ⁵¹I am the living bread that came down from heaven; whoever eats this bread will live forever; and the bread that I will give is my flesh for the life of the world."

⁵²The Jews quarreled among themselves, saying, "How can this man give us [his] flesh to eat?" ⁵³Jesus said to them, "Amen, amen, I say to you, unless you eat the flesh of the Son of Man and drink

The sapiential theme—6:35-50

Unlike Old Testament wisdom, Jesus' teaching nourishes   Sir 24:20
37-39 forever. And just as Jesus watched that no fragments of the bread should perish (v. 12), so he watches that none of those nourished by this teaching shall perish (save only Judas, v. 70f).   Jn 17:12; 4:14
40   The heavenly bread of divine teaching has the same effect as the living water of divine teaching: eternal life (notice that Jesus draws his metaphors from ordinary life).
41   As their ancestors during the exodus murmured about the   Ex 16:2, 8
42 manna, "the Jews" murmur about this new manna. Their claim to know Jesus' origin is Johannine irony that needs not be an-
43-46 swered. Jesus only reminds them of the prophecies that   #2 promised divine teaching such as his, and that they really do not know where he is from since they have not seen his Father.   Is 54:13
49-50 They are so proud of their ancestors and of the manna in the exodus. Yet it did not stop their fathers from dying; it did not keep them faithful to God.

The sacramental theme—6:51-58

(Note: the Vulgate numbering of verses from v. 51 on is one verse ahead of other versions.) In a deeper sense, the life-giving and, indeed, *living* bread is Jesus' own flesh. Here John gives

his blood, you do not have life within you. [54]Whoever eats my flesh and drinks my blood has eternal life, and I will raise him on the last day. [55]For my flesh is true food, and my blood is true drink. [56]Whoever eats my flesh and drinks my blood remains in me and I in him. [57]Just as the living Father sent me and I have life because of the Father, so also the one who feeds on me will have life because of me. [58]This is the bread that came down from heaven. Unlike your ancestors who ate and still died, whoever eats this bread will live forever." [59]These things he said while teaching in the synagogue in Capernaum.

The Words of Eternal Life. [60]Then many of his disciples who were listening said, "This saying is hard; who can accept it?" [61]Since Jesus knew that his disciples were murmuring about this, he said to them, "Does this shock you? [62]What if you were to see the Son of Man ascending to where he was before? [63]It is the spirit that gives life, while the flesh is of no avail. The words I have spoken to you are spirit and life. [64]But there are some of you who do not believe." Jesus knew from the beginning the ones who would not believe and the one who would betray him. [65]And he said, "For this reason I have told you that no one can come to me unless it is granted him by my Father."

[66]As a result of this, many [of] his disciples returned to their former way of life and no longer accompanied him. [67]Jesus

52 what seems to be a variant of the words of the institution of the eucharist: "The bread that I will give is my flesh for the life of the world" (cf. "This is my body given for you"). If for Paul the eucharist proclaims the death of the Lord until he 54-56 comes at the end of the world, in John the emphasis is that the Word has become flesh and has given up his flesh and blood as the food of life: *a proclamation of the incarnation as salvi-* 58 *fic* (the blood is definitely a Last Supper theme). The sacramental theology here is truly profound; namely, if baptism gives us that life which the Father shares with the Son, the eucharist is food nourishing it.

Lk 22:19; cf. Jn 3:16 1 Cor 11:26

Reaction to Jesus' words—6:59-71

59 The synagogue of Capernaum, well known from the Synoptics, has been the scene of Jesus' teaching. (And later a synagogue may have been the site for debates between "the Jews" and Johannine Christians over the true bread from heaven.)
60-61 Jesus' words are greeted with unbelief. In answer he refers to his glorification (ascent to heaven by way of the cross) as the event which will give credence to his teaching (and reality to 63 the eucharist), for when he is glorified, he will give the Spirit. And it is this Holy Spirit that gives life. Their materialistic quest is after bread (the flesh level; as with Nicodemus, flesh is opposed to spirit) which will not give life; Jesus' teaching confers the Spirit who in turn gives life (spirit and life are a virtual 64-65 hendiadys). Those not called by his Father turn away; but

Mk 1:21-22

Cf. Jn 3:13

Jn 7:39

Jn 3:6

Cf. Jn 1:13

then said to the Twelve, "Do you also want to leave?" 68Simon Peter answered him, "Master, to whom shall we go? You have the words of eternal life. 69We have come to believe and are convinced that you are the Holy One of God." 70Jesus answered them, "Did I not choose you twelve? Yet is not one of you a devil?" 71He was referring to Judas, son of Simon the Iscariot; it was he who would betray him, one of the Twelve.

7 The Feast of Tabernacles. 1After this, Jesus moved about within Galilee; but he did not wish to travel in Judea, because the Jews were trying to kill him. 2But the Jewish feast of Tabernacles was near. 3So his brothers said to him, "Leave here and go to Judea, so that your disciples also may see the works you are doing. 4No one works in secret if he wants to be known publicly. If you do these things, manifest yourself to the world." 5For his brothers did not believe in him. 6So Jesus said to them, "My time is not yet here, but the time is always right for you. 7The world cannot hate you, but it hates me, because I testify to it that its works are evil. 8You go up to the feast. I am not going up to this feast, because my time has not yet been fulfilled." 9After he had said this, he stayed on in Galilee.

10But when his brothers had gone up to the feast, he himself also went up, not openly but [as it were] in secret. 11The Jews were looking for him at the feast and saying, "Where is he?" 12And there was considerable murmuring about him in the crowds. Some said, "He is a good man,"

67-69 Peter confesses his faith as a spokesman for the disciples (combine this with 1:42 and compare to Mt 16:15-18). Judas se-
70-71 cretly refuses faith in Jesus, an example of the ever-present dia-
bolic opposition. We may have here another element from the
Last Supper; in Luke mention of Judas' betrayal immediately
follows the institution of the eucharist.

#8a
Mk
8:32-33

Lk
22:21-23
#8a

The feast of Tabernacles—7:1-13

The approach of Tabernacles (one of the feasts on which Jews
from outside Jerusalem went up to the Holy City) raises the
question of whether or not Jesus will go to Jerusalem despite
3-5 the danger awaiting him there. His brothers (or male relatives)
show no faith in him; now they wish him to work miracles
in Judea so people will be astounded and believe. Not at all
6-8 interested in human praise, Jesus answers in a phrase with twofold meaning. His time (the hour of glorification by return to
his Father) is not now; therefore he will not *go up* (i.e., *on the
cross*—the inevitable result of showing his glory in Jerusalem).
9-10 The seeming contradiction of subsequently "going up" exists
11-13 only for those who miss this play on words. The division that
exists among the crowd about Jesus is typically Johannine:
Jesus' very presence constitutes judgment.

Mk 6:3;
3:21, 31

Second
tempta-
tion;
Mt 4:5-6
#3a
Cf. Jn 2:4

#5

The discourse at Tabernacles takes on added overtones if
we are familiar with the ceremonies of this week-long feast
(with an added eighth day) celebrated in September/October
at the fall harvest in order to pray for early rain in the winter

Dt
16:13-16;
Lv
23:34-43

[while] others said, "No; on the contrary, he misleads the crowd." [13]Still, no one spoke openly about him because they were afraid of the Jews.

The First Dialogue. [14]When the feast was already half over, Jesus went up into the temple area and began to teach. [15]The Jews were amazed and said, "How does he know scripture without having studied?" [16]Jesus answered them and said, "My teaching is not my own but is from the one who sent me. [17]Whoever chooses to do his will shall know whether my teaching is from God or whether I speak on my own. [18]Whoever speaks on his own seeks his own glory, but whoever seeks the glory of the one who sent him is truthful, and there is no wrong in him. [19]Did not Moses give you the law? Yet none of you keeps the law. Why are you trying to kill me?" [20]The crowd answered, "You are possessed! Who is trying to kill you?" [21]Jesus answered and said to them, "I performed one work and all of you are amazed [22]because of it. Moses gave you circumcision—not that it came from Moses but rather from the patriarchs— and you circumcise a man on the sabbath. [23]If a man can receive circumcision on a sabbath so that the law of Moses may not be broken, are you angry with me because I made a whole person well on a sabbath? [24]Stop judging by appearances, but judge justly."

[25]So some of the inhabitants of Jerusalem said, "Is he not the one they are trying to kill? [26]And look, he is speaking openly and they say nothing to him. Could the authorities have realized that he is the Messiah? [27]But we know where

season. We might note these aspects of the feast: (a) the people lived in huts or bowers to recall their ancestors' sojourn in the desert; (b) to symbolize the need for rain, there was a daily procession from the pool of Siloam bringing water as a libation to the Temple; (c) the court of the women in the Temple was lighted by immense torches.

Za
14:16-21

At the middle of the feast—7:14-36

The appearance of the Galilean teacher provokes amazement. How is he able to teach without ever having a master? Again and again in the rabbinic literature we hear the Jewish teachers
16-18 quoting their masters: "Rabbi So and So says. . . ." Jesus answers that he does have a master: the Father whose glory he
19-20 seeks and whose word he conveys. Then Jesus returns to the incident of his last appearance in Jerusalem (a year and a half before?) when the Jews sought to kill him because he healed
21-24 on the Sabbath. He now justifies his action on more humanitarian grounds; for if they could circumcise on the Sabbath, an action affecting only a part of the body, why could he not deal with the whole body? As mentioned, this type of argument is seen in the Synoptics, as is also the accusation that Jesus had
demoniacal power.

Cf. Jn
5:10-18

Mk 3:4, 22

25-27 Once again Jesus divides his hearers. Some object to him on grounds of contemporary messianic expectation. The Messiah, when he would come, was supposed to remain hidden,

he is from. When the Messiah comes, no one will know where he is from." ²⁸So Jesus cried out in the temple area as he was teaching and said, "You know me and also know where I am from. Yet I did not come on my own, but the one who sent me, whom you do not know, is true. ²⁹I know him, because I am from him, and he sent me." ³⁰So they tried to arrest him, but no one laid a hand upon him, because his hour had not yet come. ³¹But many of the crowd began to believe in him, and said, "When the Messiah comes, will he perform more signs than this man has done?"

Officers Sent to Arrest Jesus. ³²The Pharisees heard the crowd murmuring about him to this effect, and the chief priests and the Pharisees sent guards to arrest him. ³³So Jesus said, "I will be with you only a little while longer, and then I will go to the one who sent me. ³⁴You will look for me but not find [me], and where I am you cannot come." ³⁵So the Jews said to one another, "Where is he going that we will not find him? Surely he is not going to the dispersion among the Greeks to teach the Greeks, is he? ³⁶What is the meaning of his saying, 'You will look for me and not find [me], and where I am you cannot come'?"

Rivers of Living Water. ³⁷On the last and greatest day of the feast, Jesus stood up and exclaimed, "Let anyone who thirsts come to me and drink. ³⁸Whoever believes in me, as scripture says:
'Rivers of living water will flow from within him.'"
³⁹He said this in reference to the Spirit that those who came to believe in him were

28-29 and unknown till Elijah revealed him to the world. But the Galilean village background of Jesus was well known. (Again there is irony in the reference to Jesus' origin.) Others are convinced by his signs. #2

32 The Pharisees interfere by sending the Temple police to arrest him. (This incident breaks off and is not taken up again till v. 45, which is technically four days later—an obviously artificial arrangement.) Jesus warns "the Jews" that they have but a short time to accept him; like wisdom he can be found only by those who sincerely search. The sneering Jewish retort about going to teach the Gentiles exemplifies Johannine irony, for that is precisely what Jesus will do in his church. Cf. p. 15 / Is 55:6; Dt 4:29; Wis 6:13; Prv 1:28-29 #2

33-34
35

On the last day of the feast—7:37-52

The crowds have watched the daily water ceremony made with petitions for rain; yet the real source of water from heaven stands in their midst. The best reading for verses 37-38 is:

37-38
If anyone THIRST, let him *come to me;*
and let him DRINK who *believes in me;*
As the Scripture says,
'From within him there shall flow
rivers of living water.' Ps 78:15-16, 24; 105:40-41; Is 48:21; 12:3

As Moses struck the rock in the desert to get water during the exodus, so Jesus, the rock of the new Israel, gives living water. Ex 17:6 / 1 Cor 10:4

to receive. There was, of course, no Spirit yet, because Jesus had not yet been glorified.

Discussion about the Origins of the Messiah. ⁴⁰Some in the crowd who heard these words said, "This is truly the Prophet." ⁴¹Others said, "This is the Messiah." But others said, "The Messiah will not come from Galilee, will he? ⁴²Does not scripture say that the Messiah will be of David's family and come from Bethlehem, the village where David lived?" ⁴³So a division occurred in the crowd because of him. ⁴⁴Some of them even wanted to arrest him, but no one laid hands on him.

⁴⁵So the guards went to the chief priests and Pharisees, who asked them, "Why did you not bring him?" ⁴⁶The guards answered, "Never before has anyone spoken like this one." ⁴⁷So the Pharisees answered them, "Have you also been deceived? ⁴⁸Have any of the authorities or the Pharisees believed in him? ⁴⁹But this crowd, which does not know the law, is accursed." ⁵⁰Nicodemus, one of their members who had come to him earlier, said to them, ⁵¹"Does our law condemn a person before it first hears him and finds out what he is doing?" ⁵²They answered and said to him, "You are not from Galilee also, are you? Look and see that no prophet arises from Galilee."

A Woman Caught in Adultery. [⁵³Then each went to his own house,

8 ¹while Jesus went to the Mount of Olives. ²But early in the morning he

39 And the water is the Spirit to be given in baptism when Jesus has returned to his Father from the cross.

40 Because Jesus fulfills the role of a new Moses, some see in
41-42 him the prophet-like-Moses. Others again object to his Galilean origin in that it contradicts the promised Davidic origin of the Messiah. (The ironical silence of John on this charge *may* show awareness of the Synoptic tradition of Jesus' birth in Bethlehem which the reader is expected to know). Picking up the
45 story of the Pharisees' envoys (v. 32), we find that just as
46 Jesus' *signs* convinced some in v. 31, his *words* convince the
47 Temple police here. With contempt for the religiously unobservant, of which we have an echo in rabbinic documents,
48-49 the leaders claim that Jesus has not convinced anyone who
50-52 was educated. The timid Nicodemus is the living proof that in claiming knowledge they are ignorant, but his plea for justice is met with contempt.

Jn 19:34; 20:22; 1 Cor 12:13 Cf. Jn 1:21; 4:19

[The adulteress episode—7:53–8:11

This story is missing from the best Greek manuscripts. While for Catholics it is canonical and inspired, almost certainly it is out of context here. Some manuscripts place it in Luke among the cunning questions presented to Jesus during Holy Week; this would be a far better setting. The story's illustration of themes in Jn 8:15 and 46 probably accounts for its present position. The Greek style is closer to Luke than to John. We may have here an old story about Jesus preserved by a hand other than that which gave us the rest of the Gospel.

after Lk 21:38 Lk 20: 20-40

arrived again in the temple area, and all the people started coming to him, and he sat down and taught them. ³Then the scribes and the Pharisees brought a woman who had been caught in adultery and made her stand in the middle. ⁴They said to him, "Teacher, this woman was caught in the very act of committing adultery. ⁵Now in the law, Moses commanded us to stone such women. So what do you say?" ⁶They said this to test him, so that they could have some charge to bring against him. Jesus bent down and began to write on the ground with his finger. ⁷But when they continued asking him, he straightened up and said to them, "Let the one among you who is without sin be the first to throw a stone at her." ⁸Again he bent down and wrote on the ground. ⁹And in response, they went away one by one, beginning with the elders. So he was left alone with the woman before him. ¹⁰Then Jesus straightened up and said to her, "Woman, where are they? Has no one condemned you?" ¹¹She replied, "No one, sir." Then Jesus said, "Neither do I condemn you. Go, [and] from now on do not sin any more."]

The Light of the World. ¹²Jesus spoke to them again, saying, "I am the light of the world. Whoever follows me will not walk in darkness, but will have the light of life." ¹³So the Pharisees said to him, "You testify on your own behalf, so your testimony cannot be verified." ¹⁴Jesus answered and said to them, "Even if I do testify on my own behalf, my testimony can be verified, because I know where I came from and where I am going. But you do not know where I come from or where I am going. ¹⁵You judge by appearances, but I do not judge anyone. ¹⁶And even if I should judge, my judgment is valid, because I am not alone, but it is I and the Father who sent me. ¹⁷Even in your law it is written that the testimony of two men can be verified. ¹⁸I testify on my behalf and so does the Father who sent me." ¹⁹So

1-2 As during Holy Week, Jesus spends the night on the Mount of Olives and teaches daily in the Temple. The problem that the Pharisees present him is somewhat like that of Caesar's coin in Luke. If he authorizes death, he violates Roman law, which did not allow the Jews to administer capital punishment. If he advises mercy, he violates Mosaic law. As with the coin, Jesus' answer puts the burden back on his questioners. Not being able to claim freedom from sin, the Pharisees slip off, leaving the sinner and the Sinless alone (Augustine: *Relicti sunt duo, misera et misericordia*). Although he has the right, he will not condemn either, for he judges no one.]

3-6 *Lk 21:37-38*
7 *Lk 20:21-25 / Jn 18:31 / Lv 20:10*
9 *Jn 8:46; Heb 4:15*
11 *Jn 8:15*

A composite discourse—8:12-29

Returning to the Tabernacles setting, we find Jesus claiming that he, and not the festal torch, is the real light of the world (a theme to be resumed in c. 9). Actually the following verses in c. 8 seem to duplicate verses found elsewhere in John. The theme of *witness* and *judgment* we have seen in c. 5. That whoever knows Jesus knows his Father is the Johannine theme of unity between Father and Son. His hearers ask for the Father while the only real image of the Father is standing be-

#7 Jn 5:31ff, 22-23 / Jn 12:45; 14:9

they said to him, "Where is your father?" Jesus answered, "You know neither me nor my Father. If you knew me, you would know my Father also." ²⁰He spoke these words while teaching in the treasury in the temple area. But no one arrested him, because his hour had not yet come.

Jesus, the Father's Ambassador. ²¹He said to them again, "I am going away and you will look for me, but you will die in your sin. Where I am going you cannot come." ²²So the Jews said, "He is not going to kill himself, is he, because he said, 'Where I am going you cannot come'?" ²³He said to them, "You belong to what is below, I belong to what is above. You belong to this world, but I do not belong to this world. ²⁴That is why I told you that you will die in your sins. For if you do not believe that I AM, you will die in

your sins." ²⁵So they said to him, "Who are you?" Jesus said to them, "What I told you from the beginning. ²⁶I have much to say about you in condemnation. But the one who sent me is true, and what I heard from him I tell the world." ²⁷They did not realize that he was speaking to them of the Father. ²⁸So Jesus said [to them], "When you lift up the Son of Man, then you will realize that I AM, and that I do nothing on my own, but I say only what the Father taught me. ²⁹The one who sent me is with me. He has not left me alone, because I always do what is pleasing to him." ³⁰Because he spoke this way, many came to believe in him.

Jesus and Abraham. ³¹Jesus then said to those Jews who believed in him, "If you remain in my word, you will truly be my disciples, ³²and you will know the truth, and the truth will set you free." ³³They

---

20   fore their eyes. (The treasury as the site of Jesus' teaching is   Mk 12:41
21-22 found in Mark.) The statement that Jesus will go away appears
       again; and again there is Johannine irony in the Jewish reply,   Jn 7:33ff
       "Will he kill himself?" for he will voluntarily lay down his life   #2
       for others.   Jn 10:18

       As with Nicodemus, Jesus insists that he is not from this   Jn 3:31
24   world but from above. The only thing that can save "the Jews"
       is belief that HE IS (the divine name "I am"). The Jews ask   Cf. Jn 6:20
25   who he is. His answer is of uncertain meaning; some prefer
       "Why do I speak to you at all!"; but "What I told you from
       the beginning" is favored by the Bodmer papyrus. Then Jesus   Cf. p. 9
26   returns rather abruptly to the judgment theme of v. 16. The   P66
28   climax of the address is the second reference in John to the Son
       of Man's being lifted up in the process of return to the Father,   Cf. Jn
       from whom he has never really been separated.   3:13-15

Abraham and Jesus—8:30-59

The reference to "Jews" who believe in Jesus (and will soon try to kill him) is noteworthy. Here as in 6:61-65 John may be attacking "Christians" whose minimalist christology is com-
32   parable to Jewish disbelief. Jesus claims that his doctrine is true and will free people from sin (remember the Pauline doctrine
33   that Christ has freed us from the Mosaic Law). "The Jews" mis-   Gal 4:22-31
       understand him to speak of political freedom, and boast that   #1

answered him, "We are descendants of Abraham and have never been enslaved to anyone. How can you say, 'You will become free'?" ³⁴Jesus answered them, "Amen, amen, I say to you, everyone who commits sin is a slave of sin. ³⁵A slave does not remain in a household forever, but a son always remains. ³⁶So if a son frees you, then you will truly be free. ³⁷I know that you are descendants of Abraham. But you are trying to kill me, because my word has no room among you. ³⁸I tell you what I have seen in the Father's presence; then do what you have heard from the Father."

³⁹They answered and said to him, "Our father is Abraham." Jesus said to them, "If you were Abraham's children, you would be doing the works of Abraham. ⁴⁰But now you are trying to kill me, a man who has told you the truth that I heard from God; Abraham did not do this. ⁴¹You are doing the works of your father!" [So] they said to him, "We are not illegitimate. We have one Father, God." ⁴²Jesus said to them, "If God were your Father, you would love me, for I came from God and am here; I did not come on my own, but he sent me. ⁴³Why do you not understand what I am saying? Because you cannot bear to hear my word. ⁴⁴You belong to your father the devil and you willingly carry out your father's desires. He was a murderer from the beginning and does not stand in truth, because there is no truth in him. When he tells a lie, he speaks in character, because he is a liar and the father of lies. ⁴⁵But because I speak the truth, you do not believe me. ⁴⁶Can any of you charge me with sin? If I am telling the truth, why do you not believe me? ⁴⁷Whoever belongs to God hears the words of God; for this reason you do not listen, because you do not belong to God."

⁴⁸The Jews answered and said to him, "Are we not right in saying that you are a Samaritan and are possessed?" ⁴⁹Jesus answered, "I am not possessed; I honor my Father, but you dishonor me. ⁵⁰I do not seek my own glory; there is one who seeks it and he is the one who judges. ⁵¹Amen, amen, I say to you, whoever keeps my word will never see death."

they have never been willing subjects to other nations. Pride in being "sons of Abraham" is an authentic Synoptic theme. | Mt 3:9

34 Jesus replies by stressing the spiritual nature of freedom. As | Rom 6:17
35-36 the only real Son of God, he is the master in his Father's house; | Heb 3:5-6
only he can emancipate the slaves by delivering them from | Rom 8:2
37-40 sin. Physical descent from Abraham is of no avail. A true son | Mt 8:11-12
acts like his father. Abraham believed when God spoke to | Gn 15:6 / Mal 2:10
41 him; they do not, and so they are illegitimate. When they | 1 Jn 4:6
42-43 retort that they are of God, Jesus denies it. He should know | Gn 3:4-5, 19
44 for he has come from God. Rather they are of the devil, who | Wis 2:24
lied in the Garden of Eden and brought death into the world | Mt 12:34;
45-47 through sin; and they are liars like their father. That is why | 1 Jn 2:22; 5:10
they cannot recognize the truth.

48 They repeat the accusation of diabolic possession ("Samari- | Jn 7:20
tan"—Samaria was famous for magicians like Simon Magus,
49-50 but the charge may reflect the presence of Samaritans in the
Johannine community). Jesus warns that such blasphemy will | Jn 4:39
51 be avenged by the Father, jealous for his Son's honor. As the | Acts 8:9
life, Jesus can deliver from death, the kingdom of the devil.

⁵²[So] the Jews said to him, "Now we are sure that you are possessed. Abraham died, as did the prophets, yet you say, 'Whoever keeps my word will never taste death.' ⁵³Are you greater than our father Abraham, who died? Or the prophets, who died? Who do you make yourself out to be?" ⁵⁴Jesus answered, "If I glorify myself, my glory is worth nothing; but it is my Father who glorifies me, of whom you say, 'He is our God.' ⁵⁵You do not know him, but I know him. And if I should say that I do not know him, I would be like you a liar. But I do know him and I keep his word. ⁵⁶Abraham your father rejoiced to see my day; he saw it and was glad." ⁵⁷So the Jews said to him, "You are not yet fifty years old and you have seen Abraham?" ⁵⁸Jesus said to them, "Amen, amen, I say to you, before Abraham came to be, I AM." ⁵⁹So they picked up stones to throw at him; but Jesus hid and went out of the temple area.

9 **The Man Born Blind.** ¹As he passed by he saw a man blind from birth. ²His disciples asked him, "Rabbi, who sinned, this man or his parents, that he was born blind?" ³Jesus answered, "Neither he nor his parents sinned; it is so that the works of God might be made visible through him. ⁴We have to do the works of the one who sent me while it is day. Night is coming when no one can work. ⁵While I am in the world, I am the light

52-53 When they object that freedom from death was not granted **54-58** even to the greatest like Abraham, Jesus clearly claims to be greater than Abraham, using once again the divine name "I AM." (The reference to Abraham's seeing Jesus' "day" may mean that in the birth of Isaac, Abraham had seen the fulfillment of the promise of a messianic line. The rabbis interpreted **59** his laughter on that occasion as joy.) "The Jews" understand the reference to divinity, and try to kill him for blasphemy.

Ex 3:13-14

Gn 17:16-17

Lv 24:16

Light to the blind; blindness to those who claim to see—9:1-41

We now return to the light-theme of Tabernacles (8:12). Isaiah had predicted that the Messiah would be a light to the nations and would open eyes that are blind. The present chapter is a unit illustrating this. An ironical contrast is shown between the man who was blind but came to sight because of Jesus, and the Pharisees or "the Jews," who could see and were brought to blindness because of Jesus. The blind man knows little and yet learns much; the Pharisees know everything and can be taught nothing.

Is 42:6-7; 29:18; 49:6

Jn 9:12, 25, 36

Jn 9:16, 24, 29

The cure of the man born blind—9:1-7

Notice the emphasis on the man being blind *from birth*. We shall see a possible reference to baptism, and Augustine related the blindness to original sin ("This blind man is the human **2-3** race"). Jesus refuses to attribute illness to sin despite the belief that it was a punishment implying guilt. The only blindness that necessarily presupposes sin is blindness of the will. So

Lk 13:2

of the world." ⁶When he had said this, he spat on the ground and made clay with the saliva, and smeared the clay on his eyes, ⁷and said to him, "Go wash in the Pool of Siloam" (which means Sent). So he went and washed, and came back able to see.

⁸His neighbors and those who had seen him earlier as a beggar said, "Isn't this the one who used to sit and beg?" ⁹Some said, "It is," but others said, "No, he just looks like him." He said, "I am." ¹⁰So they said to him, "[So] how were your eyes opened?" ¹¹He replied, "The man called Jesus made clay and anointed my eyes and told me, 'Go to Siloam and wash.'

So I went there and washed and was able to see." ¹²And they said to him, "Where is he?" He said, "I don't know."

¹³They brought the one who was once blind to the Pharisees. ¹⁴Now Jesus had made clay and opened his eyes on a sabbath. ¹⁵So then the Pharisees also asked him how he was able to see. He said to them, "He put clay on my eyes, and I washed, and now I can see." ¹⁶So some of the Pharisees said, "This man is not from God, because he does not keep the sabbath." [But] others said, "How can a sinful man do such signs?" And there was a division among them. ¹⁷So they said to the blind man again, "What do you have

5 that the real message of his miracle will not be lost, Jesus proclaims that he is the light of the world. His ministry is the period of light; darkness will have its hour when he is betrayed and put to death. **Jn 13:30; Lk 22:53**

6 Both of his actions preliminary to the miracle violate the rabbinic rules for the Sabbath, healing with spittle and kneading the clay. (Mark tells of Jesus using spittle on a blind man and on a deaf man. The latter incident with its "Ephpheta" has become part of our baptismal liturgy. We might wonder if the *anointing* [smearing] of the eyes with clay in John is likewise **Mk 8:23; 7:33-34**

7 connected with the anointing at baptism.) The healing itself, however, is accomplished by washing in the pool of Siloam (Hebrew: Shiloh). This pool, bearing a name interpreted as "sent," stands, in John, for Jesus, who is the one *sent* by the Father. It is John's emphasis on the symbolic meaning of the pool that suggested to Tertullian and St. Augustine a baptismal reference in addition to the obvious meaning of light healing blindness. In early catacomb art, the healing of the blind man is a symbol of baptism. **#3b**

Three interrogations—9:8-41

We follow the man as he is interrogated by his neighbors (8-12), the Pharisees (13-34), and Jesus (35-41). At each step he

8-12 learns more of Jesus. To his neighbors' questions he knows

13-15 only the man called Jesus. When the Pharisees press him,

16 he knows that Jesus is a prophet. As usual, Jesus' action produces a division among the Pharisees: John's theme of judgment here and now. The story so far runs parallel to that of **Lk 7:16**

#5

to say about him, since he opened your eyes?" He said, "He is a prophet."

[18]Now the Jews did not believe that he had been blind and gained his sight until they summoned the parents of the one who had gained his sight. [19]They asked them, "Is this your son, who you say was born blind? How does he now see?" [20]His parents answered and said, "We know that this is our son and that he was born blind. [21]We do not know how he sees now, nor do we know who opened his eyes. Ask him, he is of age; he can speak for himself." [22]His parents said this because they were afraid of the Jews, for the Jews had already agreed that if anyone acknowledged him as the Messiah, he would be expelled from the synagogue. [23]For this reason his parents said, "He is of age; question him."

[24]So a second time they called the man who had been blind and said to him, "Give God the praise! We know that this man is a sinner." [25]He replied, "If he is a sinner, I do not know. One thing I do know is that I was blind and now I see." [26]So they said to him, "What did he do to you? How did he open your eyes?" [27]He answered them, "I told you already and you did not listen. Why do you want to hear it again? Do you want to become his disciples, too?" [28]They ridiculed him and said, "You are that man's disciple; we are disciples of Moses! [29]We know that God spoke to Moses, but we do not know where this one is from." [30]The man answered and said to them, "This is what is so amazing, that you do not know where he is from, yet he opened my eyes. [31]We know that God does not listen to sinners, but if one is devout and does his will, he listens to him. [32]It is unheard of that anyone ever opened the eyes of a person born blind. [33]If this man were not from God, he would not be able to do anything." [34]They answered and said to him, "You were born totally in sin, and are you trying to teach us?" Then they threw him out.

[35]When Jesus heard that they had

18   the healing of the paralytic at Bethesda (c. 5). Now, however, the Pharisees question the very reality of the healing. The
19-21   man's parents confirm the facts but avoid interpreting them (a cowardice disdained by the Johannine Christians who were   Lk 12:11 expelled from the synagogue for confessing Jesus).

24   Returning to the man himself, the Pharisees put him under oath ("Give glory to God" was an oath formula; in Johannine   Jos 7:19 irony by telling the truth the blind man actually gives the glory   #2 that "the Jews" are denying to God). The courageous sarcasm   Jn 8:49-50
25-27   of the man's answers strikes a warm chord in the reader's heart; obviously here we have a character very different from the
28-29   timid paralytic of Jn 5. Soon the Pharisees are on the defensive and resort to Moses and their old query about Jesus' ori-   Nm 12:2-8 gins. The man points out the anomaly of their uncertainty
31-33   about Jesus, just as Jesus had done with Nicodemus. The man   Jn 3:10 himself is led to the ultimate truth that Jesus is from God. Once   Is 1:15; Prv 15:29
34   again the Pharisees' resentment for the unlearned shows itself,   Jn 7:48-49 and they retort that he must be a sinner because he was born blind (verses 2-3 above).   Wis 6:17

35   Now Jesus interrogates the man, like wisdom seeking those who are worthy. In response to a (primitive baptismal?) de-

thrown him out, he found him and said, "Do you believe in the Son of Man?" [36]He answered and said, "Who is he, sir, that I may believe in him?" [37]Jesus said to him, "You have seen him and the one speaking with you is he." [38]He said, "I do believe, Lord," and he worshiped him. [39]Then Jesus said, "I came into this world for judgment, so that those who do not see might see, and those who do see might become blind."

[40]Some of the Pharisees who were with him heard this and said to him, "Surely we are not also blind, are we?" [41]Jesus said to them, "If you were blind, you would have no sin; but now you are saying, 'We see,' so your sin remains.

10 **The Good Shepherd.** [1]"Amen, amen, I say to you, whoever does not enter a sheepfold through the gate but climbs over elsewhere is a thief and a robber. [2]But whoever enters through the gate is the shepherd of the sheep. [3]The gatekeeper opens it for him, and the sheep hear his voice, as he calls his own sheep by name and leads them out. [4]When he

mand for a confession of Jesus, the man hails him as the Son of Man, the great figure seen in Daniel and the apocryphal book of Henoch. The man's faith and spontaneous worship is touching when compared with the blindness of "the Jews"; he is the true son of Abraham because he acts as Abraham acted. Jesus points out the lesson, and the Pharisees ask (Johannine irony) with a sneer if Jesus thinks they are blind. They are worse than blind; they *will* not to see. The story began with the declaration that physical blindness is not caused by sin (v. 3); it closes with the declaration that spiritual blindness is caused by sin.

36-38 *Dn 7:13ff; Hen 46, 1; 62, 9; 69, 26-29*

39-40

41 *#2*

#4

Shepherd parables—10:1-18

The connection between this section and the previous account is not as tenuous as a first glance might indicate: the Pharisees are still in view. The series of parables on the sheepfold point out how true care for the flock is exercised by Jesus, while selfish interests characterize the Pharisees. There are several different figures employed to show the same lesson; confusion will occur if we try to make one consistent allegory of them all. Background is supplied by the "shepherd" texts of the Old Testament and by the Synoptic parables dealing with shepherds and flocks. At the time other New Testament works were using "shepherd" for human pastors of the church, John is insisting on Jesus as the sole model shepherd.

1-3a The first part of the parable contrasts the shepherd and the thieves. The gatekeeper must be awake to recognize the true master of the sheep (who is the Son of Man in Luke and whom the Pharisees cannot recognize in Jn 9:35). The flock spontaneously knows his voice and follows him, even as the blind man recognized Jesus. The picture is intimately Palestinian. The

#6?

Nm 27:16-17; Ez 34

Mt 18:12; 25:32; Acts 20:28-29 1 Pt 5:2-4 Mk 14:27; Heb 13:20

Lk 12:37-40

has driven out all his own, he walks ahead of them, and the sheep follow him, because they recognize his voice. ⁵But they will not follow a stranger; they will run away from him, because they do not recognize the voice of strangers." ⁶Although Jesus used this figure of speech, they did not realize what he was trying to tell them.

⁷So Jesus said again, "Amen, amen, I say to you, I am the gate for the sheep. ⁸All who came [before me] are thieves and robbers, but the sheep did not listen to them. ⁹I am the gate. Whoever enters through me will be saved, and will come in and go out and find pasture. ¹⁰A thief comes only to steal and slaughter and destroy; I came so that they might have life and have it more abundantly. ¹¹I am the good shepherd. A good shepherd lays down his life for the sheep. ¹²A hired man, who is not a shepherd and whose sheep are not his own, sees a wolf coming and leaves the sheep and runs away, and the wolf catches and scatters them. ¹³This is because he works for pay and has no concern for the sheep. ¹⁴I am the good shepherd, and I know mine and mine know me, ¹⁵just as the Father knows me and I know the Father; and I will lay down my life for the sheep. ¹⁶I have other sheep that do not belong to this fold. These also I must lead, and they will hear my voice, and there will be one flock, one shepherd. ¹⁷This is why the Father loves me, because I lay down my life in order

sheepfold is the yard of a house or an enclosure in a field surrounded by a low stone wall. At night the shepherds who live in the tribal tents leave their sheep in these enclosures, coming in the morning to take their sheep out to pasture.

6   As often with the Synoptic parables of the kingdom, the onlookers fail to understand. Jesus then explains with several variations on the central theme. He is the door and in that
7-8   capacity serves two purposes: (a) he is the gate by which the shepherd goes to the sheep; therefore the only authentic pastors are those admitted by Jesus (of whom Peter will be a chief example for the redactor in ch. 21). The Pharisees, since they
9   do not come through Jesus, are thieves. (b) He is the gate by
10   which the sheep come into the fold and go out to pasture. Those who come through this gate will have life (Jesus is the water of life, the bread of life, the gate of life).

11   Again Jesus is the model (good) shepherd in two ways:
12-13 (a) he is willing to lay down his life for his sheep. The Pharisees are hirelings who shear the sheep but have no loyalty to them. The faithful shepherd, like David of old, protects his flock.
14-15 (b) He knows his sheep. This intimate knowledge of his flock, which involves love, is his reason for laying down his life for
16   them. And his love goes out beyond "his own sheep" of the Johannine Community to others who believe adequately in him (contrast 8:31-35). These (to be prayed for in 17:20) constitute
17   the one flock of v. 16 (Jerome read "one fold"). His glorification will make this possible, a glorification which springs from a death that no one forces on him. (Jesus' sovereignty over

Marginal references:

Mt 13:13-16
Jn 9:39

#7?

Jn 21:15-17

Ps 118:20

1 Pt 2:25
Mt 23:4, 14; 10:16

1 S 17:34-35; Za 11:7

2 Tim 2:19;
Jn 15:13

Mt 15:24

Jer 23:3-4;
Is 56:8;
Mt 8:11

to take it up again. [18]No one takes it from me, but I lay it down on my own. I have power to lay it down, and power to take it up again. This command I have received from my Father."

[19]Again there was a division among the Jews because of these words. [20]Many of them said, "He is possessed and out of his mind; why listen to him?" [21]Others said, "These are not the words of one possessed; surely a demon cannot open the eyes of the blind, can he?"

Feast of the Dedication. [22]The feast of the Dedication was then taking place in Jerusalem. It was winter. [23]And Jesus walked about in the temple area on the Portico of Solomon. [24]So the Jews gathered around him and said to him, "How long are you going to keep us in suspense? If you are the Messiah, tell us plainly." [25]Jesus answered them, "I told you and you do not believe. The works I do in my Father's name testify to me. [26]But you do not believe, because you are not among my sheep. [27]My sheep hear my voice; I know them, and they follow me. [28]I give them eternal life, and they shall never perish. No one can take them out of my hand. [29]My Father, who has given them to me, is greater than all, and no one can take them out of the Father's hand. [30]The Father and I are one."

[31]The Jews again picked up rocks to stone him. [32]Jesus answered them, "I have shown you many good works from my Father. For which of these are you trying to stone me?" [33]The Jews answered him, "We are not stoning you for a good work but for blasphemy. You, a man, are making yourself God." [34]Jesus answered them,

---

19-21   death will govern John's passion narrative.) Once again his words cause a division among his hearers.

#5

The feast of the Dedication—10:22-42

The last in the series of feasts which Jesus will reinterpret and replace is Dedication or Hanukkah, which comes around Christmas time, in the heart of winter. The feast celebrates the dedication of an altar and the reconsecration of the Temple by the Machabees after several years of desecration under the Syrian rulers (164 B.C.). Three months have elapsed since the last time-indication in John (7:2); the continuity of thought, however, is taken for granted. The question asked of Jesus is identical with that put to him in the Synoptic account of the Holy Week trial (not given in John) and so is his answer. We might notice that Jesus does not give unbelievers the same quality answers that he gives the well-disposed; with unbelievers he insists on his witnesses.

1 Mac
4:36, 59

24-25

Lk
22:66-67
#8a
Jn
4:25-26;
9:36-37

26-27   The theme of the shepherd serves to tie this section in with
28-29   the preceding (three months earlier?). No one shall ever snatch the sheep from his hands nor from his Father's. There is
30   identity of power between him and his Father because the Father has given power over all things to the Son.

Is 43:13

Jn 3:35;
13:3

31-33   The claim to equality with God causes another Jewish at-
34-36   tempt to kill Jesus for blasphemy. Using a rabbinic type of argumentation (which can appeal to the use of the same word

"Is it not written in your law, 'I said, "You are gods"'? ³⁵If it calls them gods to whom the word of God came, and scripture cannot be set aside, ³⁶can you say that the one whom the Father has consecrated and sent into the world blasphemes because I said, 'I am the Son of God'? ³⁷If I do not perform my Father's works, do not believe me; ³⁸but if I perform them, even if you do not believe me, believe the works, so that you may real-ize [and understand] that the Father is in me and I am in the Father." ³⁹[Then] they tried again to arrest him; but he escaped from their power.

⁴⁰He went back across the Jordan to the place where John first baptized, and there he remained. ⁴¹Many came to him and said, "John performed no sign, but every-thing John said about this man was true." ⁴²And many there began to believe in him.

despite its having different meanings), Jesus points out that the judges of the Old Testament were called gods because the *word* of God came to them (e.g., to Samuel). Why then do the Jews object if the term "God" is applied to the *Word*-made-flesh? We should notice that the Father has "made holy" or conse-crated Jesus—the same word the Old Testament uses for the consecration of the Temple. On this feast of Temple-altar dedi-cation and consecration, Jesus replaces the theme of the feast.

Ps 82:6 (whole verse); 1 S 15:10

Nm 7:1

Cf. Jn 2:20

37-38 Again the Jews are told to judge his claim on the basis of his works, for both flow from the one source: the Father in
39 Jesus, and Jesus in the Father. The sheep of the house of Israel still refuse to hear the voice of the shepherd, and so he leaves
40 them. As he entered the land of Israel from Bethany across the
41-42 Jordan, he now leaves the land and returns there. Outside Is-rael's confines many believe in him. The witness of John the Baptist which opened Jesus' ministry is heard echoing at its close.

Jn 14:10-11

Jn 1:28 #4

Section 4. From Death to Life and from Life to Death; Lazarus and Entry into Jerusalem (11:1–12:36)

At one stage in the development of the Fourth Gospel the public ministry of Jesus may have ended with chapter ten; ac-cordingly Jesus would cross from beyond the Jordan back to the Promised Land that he might cross from this world to the Father (it is possible that c. 13 was once directly connected to 10). But now the raising of Lazarus in cc. 11–12 supplies a tran-sition, a half-way stop between the Jordan and Jerusalem. In-deed the Lazarus miracle and its fame become the prime and immediate cause of the condemnation of Jesus. Granted this, it is startling that the Synoptic writers, who narrate in detail the events at Jerusalem leading to Jesus' death, report nothing

Cf. p. 11

Jn 13:1

11 **The Raising of Lazarus.** ¹Now a man was ill, Lazarus from Bethany, the village of Mary and her sister Martha. ²Mary was the one who had anointed the Lord with perfumed oil and dried his feet with her hair; it was her brother Lazarus who was ill. ³So the sisters sent word to him, saying, "Master, the one you love is ill." ⁴When Jesus heard this he said, "This illness is not to end in death, but is for the glory of God, that the Son of God may be glorified through it." ⁵Now Jesus loved Martha and her sister and Lazarus. ⁶So when he heard that

of the Lazarus miracle, either as an event or as a cause. In Luke, for instance, the reception of Jesus on Palm Sunday and the fury of the Pharisees are based on "all the mighty works" of Jesus. Is John placing the Lazarus miracle here as an example of such mighty works that led to Jesus' death, indeed the mightiest of all works? The net effect is the supreme irony that it was above all Jesus' gift of life that immediately led people to put him to death. Lk 19:37

Cf. p. 13

Jesus is the light, as he showed by healing the blind. More profoundly he is the life, as he shows by raising Lazarus. This miracle, the last and greatest of his (seven?) miraculous signs, is still a sign, for it remains a promise of what he will do when glorified. But it is a sign that touches very closely on reality; the natural life given here is a pledge of the supernatural life to be given by the glorified Christ. It concludes the Book of Signs and introduces the Book of Glory, for it is the proximate cause of the decision to kill Jesus and thus to glorify him.

Jesus returns to Jerusalem—11:1-16

We hear for the first time of Lazarus. The only other Lazarus in the Gospels is in Luke's parable of the rich man, and indeed the last lines of the parable sound like a commentary on John's story: "They will not believe even if someone rises from the dead." As for Mary and Martha, they are known only to Luke. Bethany (another one near Jerusalem) is for the Synoptics the Holy Week residence of Jesus. (Notice the resurrection theme in the Synoptic Holy Week.) To complete the background, Mary's identification is anticipated from chapter twelve. Lk 16:31

Lk 10:38-39
Mk 11:12;
12:18-27
#8b

3   The wording of the report sent down to Jesus at the Jordan already reveals his love for Lazarus, a theme that recurs—was Lazarus seen as a type of the Christian to whom Jesus gives life ("Beloved" was a form of address among early Christians)? Jn 11:5,
11, 36

4   At the outset Jesus states clearly the ultimate spiritual value of the miracle: it will lead to his glory (i.e., his death and all its glorious implications). The time-indications are important, for John wishes to forestall all doubt about Lazarus' death and Rom 12:19;
1 Pt 2:11
#3b

he was ill, he remained for two days in the place where he was. [7]Then after this he said to his disciples, "Let us go back to Judea." [8]The disciples said to him, "Rabbi, the Jews were just trying to stone you, and you want to go back there?" [9]Jesus answered, "Are there not twelve hours in a day? If one walks during the day, he does not stumble, because he sees the light of this world. [10]But if one walks at night, he stumbles, because the light is not in him." [11]He said this, and then told them, "Our friend Lazarus is asleep, but I am going to awaken him." [12]So the disciples said to him, "Master, if he is asleep, he will be saved." [13]But Jesus was talking about his death, while they thought that he meant ordinary sleep. [14]So then Jesus said to them clearly, "Lazarus has died. [15]And I am glad for you that I was not there, that you may believe. Let us go to him." [16]So Thomas, called Didymus, said to his fellow disciples, "Let us also go to die with him."

[17]When Jesus arrived, he found that Lazarus had already been in the tomb for four days. [18]Now Bethany was near Jerusalem, only about two miles away. [19]And many of the Jews had come to Martha and Mary to comfort them about their brother. [20]When Martha heard that Jesus was coming, she went to meet him; but Mary sat at home. [21]Martha said to Jesus, "Lord, if you had been here, my brother would not have died. [22][But] even now I know that whatever you ask of God, God will give you." [23]Jesus said to her, "Your brother will rise." [24]Martha said to him, "I know he will rise, in the resurrection on the last day." [25]Jesus told her, "I am the resurrection and the life; whoever believes in me, even if he dies, will live, [26]and everyone who lives and believes in me will never die. Do you believe this?" [27]She said to him, "Yes, Lord. I have come to believe that you are the Messiah, the Son of God, the one who is coming into the world."

7-8   the deliberate character of Jesus' actions. The suggestion of going up to Jerusalem frightens the disciples, who correctly
9-10   recognize the danger. Jesus reminds them that there is a time   Mk 10:32
limit on the presence of the light; the night of the passion is   Jn 9:4-5;
closing in.   8:12
11-14   Jesus' reference to the sleep of death is misunderstood,   #1
16   and he has to explain. The early church quite likely would have
related Thomas' words to a spiritual context such as described   Rom 6:8; 2
by Paul: "If we have died with Christ, we believe that we shall   Cor 5:14;
also live together with Christ."   Mk 8:34-35

Lazarus is restored to life—11:17-45

Having undertaken the journey of at least a day from the Jordan, they find Lazarus dead and buried. As in Luke's picture   Lk 10:40
of Martha, she is quicker than her sister to meet Jesus. Her
21-22   words bear overtones both of reproach and petition. Jesus' an-
23-24   swer promising resurrection is misunderstood to refer to the
25-26   end of the world. In explanation, Jesus says he is both the resur-   #1
rection and the life ("and the life" is doubtful); as the *resurrection*, he gives spiritual life to the physically dead, while as the
life, he does not allow spiritual death to touch those who   Mk 12:27
27   believe in him. This provokes partial faith in Martha and she

²⁸When she had said this, she went and called her sister Mary secretly, saying, "The teacher is here and is asking for you." ²⁹As soon as she heard this, she rose quickly and went to him. ³⁰For Jesus had not yet come into the village, but was still where Martha had met him. ³¹So when the Jews who were with her in the house comforting her saw Mary get up quickly and go out, they followed her, presuming that she was going to the tomb to weep there. ³²When Mary came to where Jesus was and saw him, she fell at his feet and said to him, "Lord, if you had been here, my brother would not have died." ³³When Jesus saw her weeping and the Jews who had come with her weeping, he became perturbed and deeply troubled, ³⁴and said, "Where have you laid him?" They said to him, "Sir, come and see." ³⁵And Jesus wept. ³⁶So the Jews said, "See how he loved him." ³⁷But some of them said, "Could not the one who opened the eyes of the blind man have done something so that this man would not have died?"

³⁸So Jesus, perturbed again, came to the tomb. It was a cave, and a stone lay across it. ³⁹Jesus said, "Take away the stone." Martha, the dead man's sister, said to him, "Lord, by now there will be a stench; he has been dead for four days." ⁴⁰Jesus said to her, "Did I not tell you that if you believe you will see the glory of God?" ⁴¹So they took away the stone. And Jesus raised his eyes and said, "Father, I thank you for hearing me. ⁴²I know that you always hear me; but because of the crowd here I have said this, that they may believe that you sent me." ⁴³And when he had said this, he cried out in a loud voice, "Lazarus, come out!" ⁴⁴The

confesses Jesus as the Messiah, the Son of God—Peter's confession in Mt 16:16.

Jn 6:69; 20:31

28-31 Now Mary is called on the scene followed by the mourners. (Since the lack of efficient embalming required immediate burial, the period of active mourning continued after interment.) Her words are the same as her sister's. Jesus is *troubled*

Mk 14:5

32
33 at this grief; indeed the Greek seems to imply anger (perhaps at her lack of faith, or perhaps in the presence of the suffering caused by the prince of death; see 13:21). He is invited to come

34 and see the place of death in the same words that he had used to invite his disciples to come to him, the source of life.

Jn 1:39

37 The Jews remember his power to cure the blind and wonder why he could not have helped Lazarus; they thus unconsciously bring together the two great motifs of Jesus the light

38 and Jesus the life. Again Jesus is troubled or angry in face of
39 death. That Martha's faith or, at least, understanding, is not
40 yet perfect appears in her objection; and Jesus must remind her that he is to manifest his glory in this last of his signs, even

Jn 2:11
#4

41-42 as he manifested it in the first. Jesus' prayer is scarcely a petition: he is one with the Father, and there is no suspense about the Father's hearing him.

Jn 10:30

43-44 The actual description of the miracle clearly recalls Jesus' earlier promise: "For the hour is coming in which all who are *in the tombs* shall hear his *voice* [i.e., of the Son]. And they

Jn 5:28-29

dead man came out, tied hand and foot with burial bands, and his face was wrapped in a cloth. So Jesus said to them, "Untie him and let him go."

Session of the Sanhedrin. [45]Now many of the Jews who had come to Mary and seen what he had done began to believe in him. [46]But some of them went to the Pharisees and told them what Jesus had done. [47]So the chief priests and the Pharisees convened the Sanhedrin and said, "What are we going to do? This man is performing many signs. [48]If we leave him alone, all will believe in him, and the Romans will come and take away both our land and our nation." [49]But one of them, Caiaphas, who was high priest that year, said to them, "You know nothing, [50]nor do you consider that it is better for

you that one man should die instead of the people, so that the whole nation may not perish." [51]He did not say this on his own, but since he was high priest for that year, he prophesied that Jesus was going to die for the nation, [52]and not only for the nation, but also to gather into one the dispersed children of God. [53]So from that day on they planned to kill him.

[54]So Jesus no longer walked about in public among the Jews, but he left for the region near the desert, to a town called Ephraim, and there he remained with his disciples.

The Last Passover. [55]Now the Passover of the Jews was near, and many went up from the country to Jerusalem before Passover to purify themselves. [56]They looked for Jesus and said to one another

who have done good shall *come forth* unto the *resurrection of life*" (all the italicized words are prominent in the Lazarus story). The Greek word "cry out" will be used four times in cc. 18-19 when the crowds cry out for crucifixion; note the paradox that Jesus cries out to give life while his enemies cry out to give death to Jesus. Lazarus comes forth with his burial garments, for he will need them again when he dies; Jesus will leave his garments behind.

Jn 11:17, 43, 27, 25

Jn 18:40; 19:6, 12, 15

Jn 20:5

Condemnation of Jesus by "the Jews"—11:46-53

Those who do not believe report the episode to the Sanhedrin (the chief court composed of priests, lay elders, and Pharisees).

47-48 The Sanhedrin agree that if they let Jesus continue, he will bring on destruction. Ironically, in an early Christian view it is their killing him that will end God's dwelling in the Temple ("place") and his choice of their nation; forty years after their "preventive action" the Romans will come to destroy both Temple and nation. Caiaphas, high priest *in that fateful year* of Israel's history, speaks in even more ironical, but unconscious, prophecy: one man dying *for* the people—he means "instead of"; John means "on behalf of." The decision of the Sanhedrin is death. (Is this the Johannine version of the Sanhedrin trial which the Synoptics put in Holy Week and which John omits?)

49-52

Mt 27:51

#2

Mk 14:55ff

#8a?

54-56 But Jesus, always master of his future, does not will to die before the Passover; he therefore withdraws to Ephraim (not identified with certainty). There is no time-indication in the

Jn 10:18

as they were in the temple area, "What do you think? That he will not come to the feast?" [57]For the chief priests and the Pharisees had given orders that if anyone knew where he was, he should inform them, so that they might arrest him.

12 **The Anointing at Bethany.** [1]Six days before Passover Jesus came to Bethany, where Lazarus was, whom Jesus had raised from the dead. [2]They gave a dinner for him there, and Martha served, while Lazarus was one of those reclining at table with him. [3]Mary took a liter of costly perfumed oil made from genuine aromatic nard and anointed the feet of Jesus and dried them with her hair; the house was filled with the fragrance of the oil. [4]Then Judas the Iscariot, one [of]

Fourth Gospel for the Lazarus miracle; seemingly it was between the winter feast of c. 10 and the Passover in the following spring.

The anointing at Bethany—12:1-10

The Lazarus miracle, which provoked hatred on the Pharisees' part, now occasions love from Mary. They have settled on his death; she anoints him for burial. The time-indication here (Saturday evening: six days before the following Friday-evening Passover) is hard to reconcile with the Mark-Matthew dating Mk 14:1-3 of the same event two days before Passover. (A possible solution is that John's dating is correct, and the anointing story in Mark's account is an intrusion breaking up the original sequence Mk 14:1-2, 10ff.) Luke does not have a Holy Week anointing, only a similar, earlier scene in Galilee involving a Lk 7:36-50 sinful woman. Two different stories are probably involved: (a) a real anointing at Bethany by Mary in Mark-Matthew, John; (b) a penitential act in Galilee by a sinner (originally with no anointing) in Luke. Because of the similarity of the scenes, in oral transmission the details of the one were attached to the other. There is no solid basis for identifying Mary of Bethany with the Galilean sinner or Mary of Magdala.

2   We are not told whose house is the scene of the supper (for Mark-Matthew it is at Simon the leper's); but Lazarus is present and, true to character, Martha is serving. Mark-Matthew Lk 10:40

3   tell us that Jesus' head was anointed; the anointing of the feet (unusual) and wiping them with the hair (even stranger) are Lk 7:38 details John shares with Luke where, more logically, tears are involved and not ointment. The odor filling the house may be Mk 14:9 compared to Mark-Matthew's annotation that the fame of the woman spread to the whole world. A rabbinic maxim says: "Good ointment spreads from the bedroom into the dining room, but a good name spreads from one end of the world to the other."

his disciples, and the one who would betray him, said, ⁵"Why was this oil not sold for three hundred days' wages and given to the poor?" ⁶He said this not because he cared about the poor but because he was a thief and held the money bag and used to steal the contributions. ⁷So Jesus said, "Leave her alone. Let her keep this for the day of my burial. ⁸You always have the poor with you, but you do not always have me."

⁹[The] large crowd of the Jews found out that he was there and came, not only because of Jesus, but also to see Lazarus, whom he had raised from the dead. ¹⁰And the chief priests plotted to kill Lazarus too, ¹¹because many of the Jews were turning away and believing in Jesus because of him.

The Entry into Jerusalem. ¹²On the next day, when the great crowd that had come to the feast heard that Jesus was coming to Jerusalem, ¹³they took palm branches and went out to meet him, and cried out:
"Hosanna!
Blessed is he who comes in the name of the Lord,
[even] the king of Israel."
¹⁴Jesus found an ass and sat upon it, as is written:
¹⁵"Fear no more, O daughter Zion;
see, your king comes, seated upon an ass's colt."
¹⁶His disciples did not understand this at first, but when Jesus had been glorified they remembered that these things were written about him and that they had done

4-6   Unlike the Synoptics, John identifies the source of the complaint against Mary as Judas who, he alone reports, was a thief. In God's plan the ointment had not been sold in order that
7   she would be able to anoint him today for burial. (V. 7 is better read: "The purpose was that she might keep it for . . .," since v. 3 seems to indicate it was all used, as does Mark.)   Mk 14:3
8   In rabbinic theology, while almsgiving is classified as a praiseworthy "act of justice," care for burial is counted an
9-11   "act of charity," a higher class of good works. The Lazarus theme echoes again as the belief of the crowd drives the Pharisees to further plotting.

Jesus solemnly enters Jerusalem—12:12-16

John's account of the "Palm Sunday" procession contains significant differences from that of the Synoptics. The triumph does not originate with Jesus' disciples but with the crowd. Only John mentions the branches of palm, words reminiscent of the processions that greeted the political victories of the Machabees. Again only John tells us of the crowds calling Jesus king. Thus John seems to imply that this "great crowd" (the same expression as in 6:5—a crowd that also tried to make him king) is receiving Jesus with political enthusiasm. To correct
14-15   this, Jesus acts out a prophecy; he rides a donkey to show that, like the king promised in Zechariah, he is come to bring
16   peace and salvation. The non-political nature of his kingdom will not be clear till his death and resurrection, i.e., his glorifi-

Ps 118:26

Mt 21:6-7

2 Mac 10:7

Jn 6:15

Za 9:9-10

Jn 18:36; 2:22

this for him. [17]So the crowd that was with him when he called Lazarus from the tomb and raised him from death continued to testify. [18]This was [also] why the crowd went to meet him, because they heard that he had done this sign. [19]So the Pharisees said to one another, "You see that you are gaining nothing. Look, the whole world has gone after him."

The Coming of Jesus' Hour. [20]Now there were some Greeks among those who had come up to worship at the feast. [21]They came to Philip, who was from Bethsaida in Galilee, and asked him, "Sir, we would like to see Jesus." [22]Philip went and told Andrew; then Andrew and Philip went and told Jesus. [23]Jesus answered them, "The hour has come for the Son of Man to be glorified. [24]Amen, amen, I say to you, unless a grain of wheat falls to the ground and dies, it remains just a grain of wheat; but if it dies, it produces much fruit. [25]Whoever loves his life loses it, and whoever hates his life in this world will preserve it for eternal life. [26]Whoever serves me must follow me, and where I am, there also will my servant be. The Father will honor whoever serves me.

[27]"I am troubled now. Yet what should I say? 'Father, save me from this hour'? But it was for this purpose that I came to this hour. [28]Father, glorify your name." Then a voice came from heaven, "I have glorified it and will glorify it again." [29]The crowd there heard it and said it was thun-

cation (recall a similar statement in chapter two after the cleansing of the Temple, a scene which the Synoptics place here).

End of the public ministry—12:17-36

The faith and praises of the crowd cause the Pharisees to protest that the *whole world* (Johannine irony) is following Jesus.

20 That protestation is fulfilled in the coming of the Greeks to see Jesus (these could be proselytes, or even Greek-speaking

21-22 Jews from the diaspora). As in c. 6, Philip and Andrew are the intermediaries, perhaps because these two came from Bethsaida in the predominantly Gentile territory of Philip the

24 tetrarch. Jesus' reaction to the Greeks' request is immediate: their coming is the sign that his mission to the house of Israel is over, his work is done. Now is his *hour* to return to his Father by death and resurrection. By this glorification his mission

24-
25a will bear fruit, and the seed planted in the hearts of the Gentiles will ripen.

25b-26 The next verses emphasize a theme familiar to the Synoptics, that of following the master to death. (Note that from this point on the discourse of Jesus has parallels in the Synoptic scene of agony in Gethsemane, an event not narrated in John.)

27-28 The thought of death troubles Jesus, as in the Synoptics it troubles him in Gethsemane. If in Mark Jesus prays to be delivered from the hour, in John he refuses such a prayer. "Glorify your name" is not unlike "Your will be done." If the Father's

29 voice is mistaken for an angel speaking, in Luke an angel will

30 come from heaven to strengthen Jesus. Yet in John the pur-

Lk 19:39
#2

Jn 6:7-10

Mt
10:38-39;
16:24-25

#8

Mk 14:34

Mk 14:35

Lk 22:43;

der; but others said, "An angel has spoken to him." ³⁰Jesus answered and said, "This voice did not come for my sake but for yours. ³¹Now is the time of judgment on this world; now the ruler of this world will be driven out. ³²And when I am lifted up from the earth, I will draw everyone to myself." ³³He said this indicating the kind of death he would die. ³⁴So the crowd answered him, "We have heard from the law that the Messiah remains forever. Then how can you say that the Son of Man must be lifted up? Who is this Son of Man?" ³⁵Jesus said to them, "The light will be among you only a little while. Walk while you have the light, so that darkness may not overcome you. Whoever walks in the dark does not know where he is going. ³⁶While you have the light, believe in the light, so that you may become children of the light."

Unbelief and Belief among the Jews. After he had said this, Jesus left and hid from them. ³⁷Although he had performed so many signs in their presence they did not believe in him, ³⁸in order that the word which Isaiah the prophet spoke might be fulfilled:

"Lord, who has believed our preaching,
  to whom has the might of the Lord
  been revealed?"

³⁹For this reason they could not believe, because again Isaiah said:

⁴⁰"He blinded their eyes
  and hardened their heart,
  so that they might not see with their eyes
  and understand with their heart and
  be converted,
  and I would heal them."

⁴¹Isaiah said this because he saw his glory and spoke about him. ⁴²Nevertheless,

pose of the voice is clearly for the people that they may see the closeness of the Father and the Son.   *Jn 11:42*

31-33 Now Jesus begins the last words of his public ministry. His work is over: he has showed the Father to "his own" and thus caused them to judge themselves. Those who reject him place themselves in the camp of the prince of this world, the great adversary of Jesus, who will be cast down as Jesus is raised up on the cross and in resurrection. Verse 32 supplies the real   *#5   Cf. Jn 3:19   Lk 22:53*
34 answer to the Gentiles. The crowd that had received Jesus as a political conqueror is puzzled by his words. Is not this Mes-
35-36 siah to stay on? But the Messiah's only answer is to stress the shortness of time: the light is not to shine much longer; night will soon darken the world. Having uttered his last plea to the world, the light hides himself.   *Jn 1:9; 13:30*

Evaluation of Jesus' work—12:37-43

Pausing here, the author comments on the failure of Jesus'   *Jn 1:11*
38 "own" to receive him. The eternal plan of God in the Scriptures is the only answer. God foresaw that people would not believe either the words or the deeds of his Suffering Servant.   *Is 53:1*
39-41 Centuries before, Isaiah had seen the glory of God in a vision,   *Cf. Jn 1:29*
and had volunteered to reveal God to His people, but God had warned him that they would not believe him. John's explanation of Jewish disbelief is a historical one; his words must not   *Is 6:1-10*

many, even among the authorities, believed in him, but because of the Pharisees they did not acknowledge it openly in order not to be expelled from the synagogue. [43]For they preferred human praise to the glory of God.

Recapitulation. [44]Jesus cried out and said, "Whoever believes in me believes not only in me but also in the one who sent me, [45]and whoever sees me sees the one who sent me. [46]I came into the world as light, so that everyone who believes in me might not remain in darkness. [47]And if anyone hears my words and does not observe them, I do not condemn him, for I did not come to condemn the world but to save the world. [48]Whoever rejects me and does not accept my words has something to judge him: the word that I spoke, it will condemn him on the last day, [49]because I did not speak on my own, but the Father who sent me commanded me what to say and speak. [50]And I know that his commandment is eternal life. So what I say, I say as the Father told me."

be misunderstood as a psychological explanation denying human freedom or culpability. If, on the one hand, it was predestined that "his own" would not believe, the real cause of that unbelief is that "the person who does evil hates the light and does not come to the light that his deeds may not be exposed."

Jn 3:20

42-43   Yet, even among the leaders, Jesus' words did not fall on completely barren ground. Their fear and human respect would not vanish until the seed of faith was watered by the blood of Jesus. Then persons like Joseph of Arimathea and Nicodemus would show themselves publicly. With these words John closes the Book of Signs (see v. 37). While his own people did not receive Jesus, there were those who did receive him. It is to these that the second half of the Gospel, the Book of Glory, will be dedicated, for they are the representatives of countless numbers from other nations and other times who will believe.

Jn 19:38

To his own he came;
yet his own people did not accept him.
But all those who did accept him
he empowered to become God's children.

Jn 1:11-12

44-50 [To the end of the Book of Signs the editor of the work has added a short speech by Jesus which makes a very fine summary of Jesus' message to the world. We have heard almost every verse of it before.]

#7

Jn 3:16-19; 8:15-16, 26

III: THE BOOK OF GLORY

13 The Washing of the Disciples' Feet.
¹Before the feast of Passover, Jesus knew that his hour had come to pass

from this world to the Father. He loved his own in the world and he loved them to the end. ²The devil had already induced Judas, son of Simon the Iscariot, to hand him over. So, during supper,

PART TWO—THE BOOK OF GLORY

Jn 13:1–20:31

Section 1. The Last Supper (13:1–17:26)

In the great cycle of Jesus' life (descent from the Father and return to the Father), the bottom of the descent and the moment when the ascent begins is now when the Son takes on himself the form of a servant (v. 16). His *hour* (v. 1) has begun. The humility and self-abasement of the Son of God is clearly the meaning of the foot-washing scene. Yet in the context of the early Christian community, there may well have been an underlying sacramental motif. Indeed, some of the liturgies (Syriac, Armenian, Spanish) and some of the Fathers see baptismal implications in the washing of the feet.

Phil 2:7

#3b

We must take a moment to discuss the time-indication given in verse one for the Last Supper: "Before the feast of Passover." The Jewish day began in the evening (the Jewish calendar was a *lunar* calendar where, naturally, evening—the domain of the moon—was the dominating factor for reckoning). For John, the Passover, the fifteenth of the month of Nisan, began Friday evening at sunset; therefore the meal of Thursday evening and the events of Good Friday were on Nisan 14. But for the Synoptics Thursday's meal was a *Passover* meal, and therefore Thursday evening already was Nisan 15. Perhaps the best solution is that John's chronology is correct. But in the meal (the evening before Passover) Jesus imitated the characteristics of the Passover meal, except the lamb, to show the connection between the eucharistic blood and the exodus. In the Synoptics, this meal with Passover overtones was simplified to a Passover meal.

Ex 12:6ff.
Lv 23:5-8;
Jn 18:28;
19:31
Mk 14:12,
17; Lk
22:15

Jesus washes his disciples' feet—13:1-17

Now that the hour so often spoken of is at hand, Jesus shows his love "to the end"—to the conclusion of his life and to the uttermost. For John and Luke the real cause behind Judas' betrayal is not avarice but Satanic instigation. Two accounts of the events of c. 13 (one stressing humility, one referring to

#3a
Jn 19:30
Lk 22:1-3
#7, 3b

2

³fully aware that the Father had put everything into his power and that he had come from God and was returning to God, ⁴he rose from supper and took off his outer garments. He took a towel and tied it around his waist. ⁵Then he poured water into a basin and began to wash the disciples' feet and dry them with the towel around his waist. ⁶He came to Simon Peter, who said to him, "Master, are you going to wash my feet?" ⁷Jesus answered and said to him, "What I am doing, you do not understand now, but you will understand later." ⁸Peter said to him, "You will never wash my feet." Jesus answered him, "Unless I wash you, you will have no inheritance with me." ⁹Simon Peter said to him, "Master, then not only my feet, but my hands and head as well." ¹⁰Jesus said to him, "Whoever has bathed has no need except to have his feet washed, for he is clean all over; so you are clean, but not all." ¹¹For he knew who would betray him; for this reason, he said, "Not all of you are clean."

¹²So when he had washed their feet [and] put his garments back on and reclined at table again, he said to them, "Do you realize what I have done for you? ¹³You call me 'teacher' and 'master,' and rightly so, for indeed I am. ¹⁴If I, therefore, the master and teacher, have washed your feet, you ought to wash one another's feet. ¹⁵I have given you a model

baptism?) may be merged, for we see some doublets: v. 27 is a doublet of v. 2; and v. 3 is another introduction paralleling

3 v. 1. The solemn stress that the following action flows from the power given Jesus by his Father reminds us of Matthew's command to baptize.

Mt 28:18-19

4-5 The washing of another's feet, begrimed by travel upon dusty roads in sandals, was a menial task not required even

6 of Jewish slaves. Such utter humiliation on the part of Jesus

7 leads Peter to object. Jesus' insistence that only later would Peter understand seems to imply more than a lesson in humility, for similar passages in John show that the full lesson of the action will not be understood until Jesus is glorified. Humility can be understood now; baptism flows only from the

8 glorified Jesus. The footwashing is so important that its omission bars one from eternal inheritance. (The word for "part" implies a portion or lot in eternal life, one of the mansions Jesus was going to prepare.)

Jn 12:16
Jn 19:34
Ap 22:19;
Col 1:12;
Jn 14:1-3

9-10 Impressed, Simon wants a thorough washing. Jesus' answer provides the key to the passage. The Greek word for "bathing" is a standard New Testament term for baptism (appearing under different translations). This verse is difficult if we rely on only a humility interpretation of the washing. But if we place the passage in the context of Christian catechesis and understand Jesus' action as a symbol of baptism, then Jesus is saying that he who is baptized needs no re-baptism (a frequent patristic explanation).

1 Cor 6:11;
Tit 3:5;
Eph 5:26;
Heb 10:22

12-16 After the washing, Jesus explains the lesson of humility. In Luke's Last Supper he gives a similar lesson. Indeed verses

to follow, so that as I have done for you, you should also do. [16]Amen, amen, I say to you, no slave is greater than his master nor any messenger greater than the one who sent him. [17]If you understand this, blessed are you if you do it. [18]I am not speaking of all of you. I know those whom I have chosen. But so that the scripture might be fulfilled, 'The one who ate my food has raised his heel against me.' [19]From now on I am telling you before it happens, so that when it happens you may believe that I AM. [20]Amen, amen, I say to you, whoever receives the one I send receives me, and whoever receives me receives the one who sent me."

Announcement of Judas' Betrayal. [21]When he had said this, Jesus was deeply troubled and testified, "Amen, amen, I say to you, one of you will betray me." [22]The disciples looked at one another, at a loss as to whom he meant. [23]One of his disciples, the one whom Jesus loved, was reclining at Jesus' side. [24]So Simon Peter nodded to him to find out whom he meant. [25]He leaned back against Jesus' chest and said to him, "Master, who is it?"

13-16 have echoes in the Synoptic public ministry and elsewhere in John, and so may be secondary here. Jesus blesses his disciples if they understand *these things* (NAB: "this") and do them. His words have a parallel in the Lucan version of Jesus' institution of the eucharist (which occurs at this point in the Synoptic accounts of the Last Supper): "Do this in memory of me." Lk 22:24-27 Mt 10:24; Jn 15:20 Lk 22:19

17

The betrayal—13:18-30

There are two sections on the betrayal by Judas, verses 18-19 and verses 21-30 (again perhaps an indication of the fusion of two accounts). The Scripture text literally refers to one "who ate my bread," even though John has not mentioned any eating of bread (another reason for suggesting that the eucharistic account once stood before v. 17). If this missing eucharistic narrative is now in 6:51, the treason of Judas in 6:71 corresponds nicely with this context. Verse 20 seems out of place here; and interestingly, it is found in Matthew in the same discourse where we find the parallel to v. 16 above. Ps 41:10 See p. 45 Mt 10:40

18

20

The second account of betrayal stays close to the Synoptics, but the roles of Peter and the beloved disciple are peculiar to John. This never-identified disciple is absent from the Synoptics. To understand this scene (as well as that of the footwashing) we should picture the diners reclining on their left sides, head propped up on an elbow, facing in toward the servers with the feet out. The beloved disciple would be reclining at Jesus' right. Reclining was required for the Passover meal, and the dipping of the morsel is reminiscent of the Passover dipping of bitter herbs into the *haroseth* sauce. Thus even in John the meal has Passover characteristics. Mk 14:17-20 Mk 14:20

23-25

26

²⁶Jesus answered, "It is the one to whom I hand the morsel after I have dipped it." So he dipped the morsel and [took it and] handed it to Judas, son of Simon the Iscariot. ²⁷After he took the morsel, Satan entered him. So Jesus said to him, "What you are going to do, do quickly." ²⁸[Now] none of those reclining at table realized why he said this to him. ²⁹Some thought that since Judas kept the money bag, Jesus had told him, "Buy what we need for the feast," or to give something to the poor. ³⁰So he took the morsel and left at once. And it was night.

The New Commandment. ³¹When he had left, Jesus said, "Now is the Son of Man glorified, and God is glorified in him. ³²[If God is glorified in him,] God will also glorify him in himself, and he will glorify him at once. ³³My children,

I will be with you only a little while longer. You will look for me, and as I told the Jews, 'Where I go you cannot come,' so now I say it to you. ³⁴I give you a new commandment: love one another. As I have loved you, so you also should love one another. ³⁵This is how all will know that you are my disciples, if you have love for one another."

Peter's Denial Predicted. ³⁶Simon Peter said to him, "Master, where are you going?" Jesus answered [him], "Where I am going, you cannot follow me now, though you will follow later." ³⁷Peter said to him, "Master, why can't I follow you now? I will lay down my life for you." ³⁸Jesus answered, "Will you lay down your life for me? Amen, amen, I say to you, the cock will not crow before you deny me three times."

27 The command given Judas shows that, even at this late
28-29 moment, Jesus is in control of his destiny. (The disciples' misunderstanding of this command is a fine literary touch.) The hour of Satan, the great adversary, is at hand; the night is clos-
30 ing in on the light, but only with Jesus' permission. Indeed, with the peculiar reference to "heel" in v. 18, reminiscent of the Genesis serpent bruising the heel of the woman's seed, John may see in a scene like this an element of the titanic struggle between the Savior and the serpent foreseen from the beginning of the human story.

Jn 10:18

Jn 9:4; Lk 22:53

Gn 3:15

Ap 12:1-5

Introduction to the Last Discourse—13:31-38

With the official permission given to Satan's agent to begin the process that would put him to death, Jesus has begun his rise to glory. The announcing of his departure, for "the Jews" a
34-35 threat, is for his disciples a tender and sorrowful farewell. His farewell gift is a new commandment (Latin *mandatum*, whence Maundy Thursday) of love for one another (note: not for outsiders)—a keepsake of Jesus' presence, the last glow of the
36-38 light of the world. The exchange with Peter supplies the last contact with the Synoptic account of the Last Supper (Luke: at the supper; Mark-Matthew: while walking to Gethsemane). Peter's reckless promise to *lay down his life* is an implicit willingness to be a good shepherd. He will fail this night, but the role of the shepherd will ultimately be his.

Jn 7:33-36; 8:21-24

1 Jn 2:7-11; 2 Jn 5-6

Lk 22:31-34; Mk 14:26-31 Jn 10:11; 21:15-19

14 Last Supper Discourses. [1]"Do not let your hearts be troubled. You have faith in God; have faith also in me. [2]In my Father's house there are many dwelling places. If there were not, would I have told you that I am going to prepare a place for you? [3]And if I go and prepare a place for you, I will come back again and take you to myself, so that where I am you also may be. [4]Where [I] am going you know the way." [5]Thomas said to him, "Master, we do not know where you are going; how can we know the way?" [6]Jesus said to him, "I am the way and the truth and the life. No one comes to the Father except through me. [7]If you know me, then you will also know my Father. From now on you do know

Jesus' Last Discourse to his disciples—14:1–17:26

Now we enter the four chapters of the Last Discourse of Jesus. Were this a word-by-word transcription of what Jesus said, a highly experienced stenographer would have been needed. Obviously John has combined actual Last Supper sayings of Jesus with material scattered through the public life to form these speeches. The speeches of the first twelve chapters are largely to unbelievers; now the Fourth Gospel turns our attention to Jesus' message for believers, gathering all such material into one place. The Synoptics have great speech complexes comprised of sayings spoken on historically different occasions, e.g., Matthew's Sermon on the Mount. Here we have a Johannine synthesis, a most sublime sermon. Poised between heaven and earth, already in the ascent to glory, Jesus speaks both as still in the world and as having left it. This atemporal, non-spatial character gives the discourse its abiding value.

Jn 16:5;
17:11

#6

Part One of the Last Discourse—14:1-31

The first of the discourse's three parts contains the most references to Jesus' imminent departure; it therefore is the most appropriate in the context of the Last Supper. After the introduction at the end of chapter thirteen, Jesus stresses the theme of departure, at the same time comforting his disciples with the promise of a return at which he will gather them to himself. This seems to refer to the parousia, one of the few examples of final eschatology in the Fourth Gospel. Thomas, speaking for the others, shows no more real understanding of where Jesus is going than did "the Jews." Not only does Thomas not know that Jesus is going to the Father, but he does not even know the way there. Jesus explains that he is the *way* to the Father because he is the incarnate *truth* about the Father and gives *life* from above to human beings. He is the sole source of knowledge about the Father.

Cf. p. 17

1-3

#5
Jn 7:35;
8:22
#1

5

6

7

Jn 6:46;
8:19

him and have seen him." [8]Philip said to him, "Master, show us the Father, and that will be enough for us." [9]Jesus said to him, "Have I been with you for so long a time and you still do not know me, Philip? Whoever has seen me has seen the Father. How can you say, 'Show us the Father'? [10]Do you not believe that I am in the Father and the Father is in me? The words that I speak to you I do not speak on my own. The Father who dwells in me is doing his works. [11]Believe me that I am in the Father and the Father is in me, or else, believe because of the works themselves. [12]Amen, amen, I say to you, whoever believes in me will do the works that I do, and will do greater ones than these, because I am going to the Father. [13]And whatever you ask in my name, I will do, so that the Father may be glorified in the Son. [14]If you ask anything of me in my name, I will do it.

The Advocate. [15]"If you love me, you will keep my commandments. [16]And I will ask the Father, and he will give you another Advocate to be with you always, [17]the Spirit of truth, which the world cannot accept, because it neither sees nor knows it. But you know it, because it remains with you, and will be in you. [18]I

8
9
10-11 Philip, another Johannine character, appears on the scene, and his misunderstanding is just as profound. Jesus' answer stresses his absolute unity with the Father; he is the revelation of the Father, and neither his words nor his works are his own.

Jn 1:18; 10:37-38; 12:45, 49

12-14 To those who believe (and are, therefore, children of God) will be given the performance of works similar to and even greater than those of the Son. All that is needed is prayer in Jesus' name, a theme familiar to the Synoptics (although only John has Jesus himself answering the prayer; normally we hear of the Father answering the prayer through Jesus' intercession).

Jn 1:12

Mk 11:23-24

Rom 8:34; 1 Jn 2:1

We now enter the Triadic section of the speech where the same theme is applied successively to the Spirit (verses 15-17), to Jesus (verses 18-22), and to the Father (verses 23-24)—the theme, namely, that if we keep the commandments, the respective divine figure will come and dwell with us.

Compare Jn 14:13-16 with Lk 11:9-10, 13

The Paraclete-Spirit—14:15-17

The condition for the gift of the Spirit is our keeping the commandments, which is, after all, the test of our love for Jesus.

1 Jn 2:4-5; 3:24

16 This is the first of two promises of the Paraclete in c. 14. Paraclete (one called alongside; NAB: "Advocate") is a legal term; it means a counsellor who supports a defendant at a trial. The Spirit, then, will be the great defender of the disciples (notice that the Spirit is *another* paraclete, for Jesus himself has been a paraclete or defender of the disciples on earth and will
17 continue to be so in heaven). The expression "Spirit of truth" is Johannine (and, interestingly enough, common in the Dead Sea Scrolls, but not in a divine sense). It means the Spirit who reveals to the world the truth about Jesus, just as Jesus revealed

Mt 10:19-20

Jn 17:11-12; 1 Jn 2:1

1 Jn 5:8

will not leave you orphans; I will come to you. ¹⁹In a little while the world will no longer see me, but you will see me, because I live and you will live. ²⁰On that day you will realize that I am in my Father and you are in me and I in you. ²¹Whoever has my commandments and observes them is the one who loves me. And whoever loves me will be loved by my Father, and I will love him and reveal myself to him." ²²Judas, not the Iscariot,

said to him, "Master, [then] what happened that you will reveal yourself to us and not to the world?" ²³Jesus answered and said to him, "Whoever loves me will keep my word, and my Father will love him, and we will come to him and make our dwelling with him. ²⁴Whoever does not love me does not keep my words; yet the word you hear is not mine but that of the Father who sent me.

²⁵"I have told you this while I am with

to the world the truth about the Father. Only those who accept Jesus can accept the Spirit.   1 Jn 4:2

Jesus—14:18-22

As at the beginning of c. 14, Jesus again consoles the disciples and predicts his return, only now not at the Second Coming but in the spiritual way of divine indwelling which will enable the Christian to understand that Jesus and the Father are one.   #5
21 Once again the observance of the commandments is the con-
22 dition of this coming. A fragment of dialogue reappears briefly   #6
as a disciple of whom we hear for the first time, Judas, "not the Iscariot" (or Jude, mentioned only in Luke's list of the   Lk 6:16;
Twelve), asks why Jesus (like the Spirit) will discriminate   Acts 1:13
against the world in showing himself.

The Father—14:23-24

The answer involves the Father's coming to dwell in the Christian, that is, the Christian who keeps Jesus' words, for Jesus' words are the Father's words. The answer is indirect, to be sure, but fundamental. The world is discriminated against because it does not love God. The presence of all three divine figures can be known only through affective knowledge, a knowledge   1 Jn 4:8
steeped in love. And one cannot love God and break his word   1 Jn 5:2-3
at the same time.

Conclusion—14:25-31

The conclusion of the speech brings the second prediction of the coming of the Paraclete. Here it is his role as teacher that is stressed, a teacher in the sense of clarifying what Jesus said. It is in this role that we trust the Paraclete to preserve Christians from error and keep them ever close to the mind of Jesus. With this final assurance Jesus grants his disciples his peace,

you. [26]The Advocate, the holy Spirit that the Father will send in my name—he will teach you everything and remind you of all that [I] told you. [27]Peace I leave with you; my peace I give to you. Not as the world gives do I give it to you. Do not let your hearts be troubled or afraid. [28]You heard me tell you, 'I am going away and I will come back to you.' If you loved me, you would rejoice that I am going to the Father; for the Father is greater than I. [29]And now I have told you this before it happens, so that when it happens you may believe. [30]I will no longer speak much with you, for the ruler of the world is coming. He has no power over me, [31]but the world must know that I love the Father and that I do just as the Father has commanded me. Get up, let us go.

15 **The Vine and the Branches.** [1]"I am the true vine, and my Father is the vine grower. [2]He takes away every branch in me that does not bear fruit, and everyone that does he prunes so that it bears more fruit. [3]You are already pruned because of the word that I spoke to you. [4]Remain in me, as I remain in you. Just as a branch cannot bear fruit on its own unless it remains on the vine, so neither can you unless you remain in me. [5]I am the vine, you are the branches. Whoever remains in me and I in him will bear much fruit, because without me you can do nothing. [6]Anyone who does not remain in me will be thrown out like a branch and wither; people will gather them and throw them into a fire and they will be burned. [7]If you remain in me and my words remain in you, ask for whatever you want and it will be done for you. [8]By this is my Father glorified, that you bear much fruit and become my disciples. [9]As the Father loves me, so I also love you. Remain in my love. [10]If you keep my

27   his *shalōm* or farewell. It is a peace based on the coming of the Spirit to be actualized on Easter night when Jesus will say: "Peace to you. Receive the Holy Spirit." It is not the peace of the world, so often only an alleviation of temporal want or stress. It is the peace of being freed from sin and united to God, 28   the only complete fulfillment of all our wants. This peace cannot be disturbed by Jesus' departure to the Father; for that return, his glorification, effects peace. "The Father is greater than I," though used by Arius, was understood by the Fathers of Jesus speaking as man. As the divine Son, the Johannine Jesus is equal to the Father in power.

  Jn 20:21-22

  Rom 5:1; 14:17

  Jn 10:28-30

30   The moment of departure is here; the enemy, the ruler of this world, stands waiting. But even now Satan is fundamentally powerless in facing Jesus, and acts only by suffrance. 31   Seemingly Jesus will allow him to triumph because that is the Father's will; but the final outcome will be the triumphant recognition of Jesus' place with his Father. With this the meal ends and the disciples rise to go (Is the "Get up, let us go" another echo of the Synoptic Gethsemane scene?). The clear indication of the end of the meal, which should logically be followed by 18:1, serves us notice that the following three chapters of discourse can scarcely be considered part of one long speech spoken historically at the Last Supper.

  Mk 14:42

  #8

commandments, you will remain in my love, just as I have kept my Father's commandments and remain in his love.

[11]"I have told you this so that my joy might be in you and your joy might be complete. [12]This is my commandment: love one another as I love you. [13]No one has greater love than this, to lay down one's life for one's friends. [14]You are my friends if you do what I command you. [15]I no longer call you slaves, because a slave does not know what his master is doing. I have called you friends, because I have told you everything I have heard from my Father. [16]It was not you who chose me, but I who chose you and appointed you to go and bear fruit that will remain, so that whatever you ask the Father in my name he may give you. [17]This I command you: love one another.

The World's Hatred. [18]"If the world hates you, realize that it hated me first. [19]If you belonged to the world, the world would love its own; but because you do not belong to the world, and I have chosen you out of the world, the world hates you. [20]Remember the word I spoke to you, 'No slave is greater than his master.' If they persecuted me, they will also persecute you. If they kept my word, they will also keep yours. [21]And they will do all these things to you on account of my name, because they do not know the one who sent me. [22]If I had not come and spo-

ken to them, they would have no sin; but as it is they have no excuse for their sin. [23]Whoever hates me also hates my Father. [24]If I had not done works among them that no one else ever did, they would not have sin; but as it is, they have seen and hated both me and my Father. [25]But in order that the word written in their law might be fulfilled, 'They hated me without cause.'

[26]"When the Advocate comes whom I will send you from the Father, the Spirit of truth that proceeds from the Father, he will testify to me. [27]And you also testify, because you have been with me from the beginning.

16 [1]"I have told you this so that you may not fall away. [2]They will expel you from the synagogues; in fact, the hour is coming when everyone who kills you will think he is offering worship to God. [3]They will do this because they have not known either the Father or me. [4]I have told you this so that when their hour comes you may remember that I told you.

Jesus' Departure; Coming of the Advocate. "I did not tell you this from the beginning, because I was with you. [5]But now I am going to the one who sent me, and not one of you asks me, 'Where are you going?' [6]But because I told you this, grief has filled your hearts. [7]But I tell you the truth, it is better for you that I go.

Duplicate of Part One—16:4-33

Again in the Last Discourse we find an instance of reporting substantially the same speech in two slightly different forms. To illustrate this clearly, we ask the reader's indulgence to skip now to c. 16 and to treat the section that is, in our opinion, a duplicate of Part One of the Last Discourse.

#7

4-6

7

The opening verses concern Jesus' departure, the sorrow of the disciples and where he is going—the same ideas that opened c. 14. Again, as in c. 14, the coming of the Paraclete-Spirit is announced twice. In c. 14 the Father gives the Spirit; in c. 16 it is Jesus who sends the Spirit. This interchange is possible because the Paraclete is representative of the Son, just as

Jn 14:1-5, 29

Jn 14:16-17

For if I do not go, the Advocate will not come to you. But if I go, I will send him to you. ⁸And when he comes he will convict the world in regard to sin and righteousness and condemnation: ⁹sin, because they do not believe in me; ¹⁰righteousness, because I am going to the Father and you will no longer see me; ¹¹condemnation, because the ruler of this world has been condemned.

¹²"I have much more to tell you, but you cannot bear it now. ¹³But when he comes, the Spirit of truth, he will guide you to all truth. He will not speak on his own, but he will speak what he hears, and will declare to you the things that are coming. ¹⁴He will glorify me, because he will take from what is mine and declare it to you. ¹⁵Everything that the Father has is mine; for this reason I told you that he will take from what is mine and declare it to you.

¹⁶"A little while and you will no longer see me, and again a little while later and you will see me." ¹⁷So some of his disciples said to one another, "What does this mean that he is saying to us, 'A little while and you will not see me, and again a little while and you will see me,' and 'Because I am going to the Father'?" ¹⁸So they said, "What is this 'little while' [of which he speaks]? We do not know what he means." ¹⁹Jesus knew that they wanted to ask him, so he said to them, "Are you discussing with one another what I said, 'A little while and you will not see me, and again a little while and you will see me'? ²⁰Amen, amen, I say to you, you will

8-11 the Son is representative of the Father. As in c. 14, this first announcement stresses the legal aspect of the Paraclete. In fact, in the trial of universal judgment, the Paraclete goes on the offense and becomes a prosecuting attorney. His activity affects the three participants in the trial: (a) the world; it has *sinned* by refusing belief; (b) Jesus; although condemned to death, he is to be posthumously vindicated and the *justice* of his cause shown; (c) Satan; he who has seemingly triumphed will be shown only to have been bringing on a downfall *prejudged* by God from all eternity.   Gn 3:15

There is a Triadic section in c. 16 as in c. 14; verses 13-15 refer to the Spirit; verses 16-22 to Jesus; verses 23-27 to the Father.

The Paraclete-Spirit—16:13-15

In the second announcement of the Spirit (in c. 16 and in c. 14), the teaching aspect is emphasized. Once more this teaching is to be nothing new. Jesus received everything from the Father; the Paraclete receives everything from Jesus.   Jn 14:26

Jesus—16:16-22

Again the theme is the return of Jesus which we saw in c. 14.   Jn 14:18-22
17-18 There is also some misunderstanding by the disciples which   Jn 16:16
is parallel to the misunderstanding of Peter and Thomas in   = 14:19
20 cc. 13-14. Jesus' answer refers to their sorrow, which is not   Jn 13:36-37; 14:5

weep and mourn, while the world rejoices; you will grieve, but your grief will become joy. ²¹When a woman is in labor, she is in anguish because her hour has arrived; but when she has given birth to a child, she no longer remembers the pain because of her joy that a child has been born into the world. ²²So you also are now in anguish. But I will see you again, and your hearts will rejoice, and no one will take your joy away from you. ²³On that day you will not question me about anything. Amen, amen, I say to you, whatever you ask the Father in my name he will give you. ²⁴Until now you have not asked anything in my name; ask and you will receive, so that your joy may be complete.

²⁵"I have told you this in figures of speech. The hour is coming when I will no longer speak to you in figures but I will tell you clearly about the Father. ²⁶On that day you will ask in my name, and

I do not tell you that I will ask the Father for you. ²⁷For the Father himself loves you, because you have loved me and have come to believe that I came from God. ²⁸I came from the Father and have come into the world. Now I am leaving the world and going back to the Father." ²⁹His disciples said, "Now you are talking plainly, and not in any figure of speech. ³⁰Now we realize that you know everything and that you do not need to have anyone question you. Because of this we believe that you came from God." ³¹Jesus answered them, "Do you believe now? ³²Behold, the hour is coming and has arrived when each of you will be scattered to his own home and you will leave me alone. But I am not alone, because the Father is with me. ³³I have told you this so that you might have peace in me. In the world you will have trouble, but take courage, I have conquered the world."

21-22 permanent (cf. 14:18), and to the rejection of the world (cf. 14:19). Here in c. 16 the theme of ultimate rejoicing is expanded by the illustration of the woman bringing forth her child—the death and resurrection of Jesus is in some ways the birth of the Messiah.

The Father—16:23-27

We now see a return of the theme of making requests in Jesus' name (only this time it is the Father who will answer the request). Jesus promises a plain revelation of the Father, and 25-27 stresses the intimacy of the Father's love for those who accept the Son.

Jn 14:13-14
Jn 14:23-24

Conclusion—16:28-33

Jesus speaks of his departure more incisively than in 14:28. Verses 29-30 have no parallel in c. 14 (although the theme of believing appears in 14:29). After all the misunderstandings, the disciples finally seem to begin to understand. The speech 32 closes on the theme of the fatal hour being at hand and the final triumph of Jesus who is ever reliant on his Father. And 33 again we find mention of peace (14:27) and the "I have told you" of 14:29.

Jn 14:30-31

The phrasing of the two accounts in cc. 14 and 16 is slightly different; but, all considered, the similarities of content and organization are too startling to be accidental.

Part Two of the Last Discourse—15:1–16:4

This section of the Last Discourse bears the closest parallels to the Synoptic speeches of Jesus' public life. Nevertheless, even #8b if many of its statements may have originally been made at another time, the Last Supper motif has permeated them and the new context has modified the message. We may subdivide the unit as follows:

(a) the vine and the branches, a metaphor expressive of the intimate *love* between Jesus and his followers: 15:1-17.

(b) the *hatred* of the world for his followers: 15:18–16:4.

The vine and the branches—15:1-8

A search for a parable in John would produce a rare and rewarding example in the passage on the vine and its branches. (Some versions have a vineyard and vines instead of a vine and branches; certainly the picture of a vineyard is more suited to v. 6. The Synoptics have several parables treating the king- Mt 20:1-8; dom of heaven as a vineyard. As we have already observed, 21:33-41 in John the person of Jesus is equivalent to the kingdom of heaven in the Synoptics.) In the Old Testament, Israel is frequently pictured as God's choice vine (or vineyard), one that Hos 10:1; he has nurtured with consummate care, only to receive bitter Is 5:1-7; fruit. We have seen Jesus replacing Jewish institutions and $\frac{\text{Ez 17:5-}}{10; \text{Ps}}$ 1 feasts; now he shows himself as the vine of the New Israel. 80:9-17 In union with him, Christians of the New Israel will bear only fruit that is pleasing to the vine-dresser, God. In the Old Mt 7:17-20 2-6 Testament, God often threatened to prune or even uproot the unproductive vine. While the vine of the New Israel will not $\frac{\text{Mt 13:30,}}{40\text{-}42,}$ fail, there will be fallen branches to be removed and burned. 15:13

We might note that Jesus as the vine is another echo of Jesus as divine wisdom, for wisdom is also compared to a vine. Jesus, $\frac{\text{Sir}}{24:17\text{-}18}$ who at Cana was reluctant to produce an abundance of wine until his hour would come, is now the true vine transmitting life to the branches. The *Didache*, which gives us the earliest account of the eucharist outside the New Testament, has this blessing over the chalice: "We thank you, our Father, for the holy vine of David, your servant, that you have revealed through Jesus Christ, your servant."

Abiding love—15:9-17

The themes of divine indwelling, asking in Jesus' name, keeping the commandments, and abiding love (all of which we saw in Part I) are touched on in verses 7-10. Jesus' joy which is promised here is like Jesus' peace; it will come in its fulness only after the resurrection. We hear again of the supreme commandment of loving one another (a restriction to Jesus' followers) and the theme of laying down one's life. Jesus' laying down his life is not only the supreme example of love; as an exemplary cause, it is what makes love peculiarly Christian. Abraham, the Old Testament ideal, was the friend of God; the New Testament ideal is to be the friend of or one loved by Jesus. Although Jesus has in the past called the disciples servants, what he has revealed to them raises them to the rank of friends; for indeed their knowledge of God now outshines that of any Israelitic figure. Jesus has chosen the recipients of this revelation. The return for this disinterested manifestation of God's love should be their love toward fellow disciples.

Marginal references: 11 — Cf. Jn 14:27; Jn 20:20-21; Jn 13:34-35, 37. 12 — . 13 — 1 Jn 3:16. 14-15 — Is 41:8; Jas 2:23; Jn 12:26; 13:16; Eph 3:5. 16-17 — 1 Jn 4:10-11; Mt 5:43-48.

The world's hatred—15:18-16:4

The Father testified to his love for the Son by sending him into the world; the Son testifies to his love for the disciples by sending them into the world. It is this mission of the disciples that arouses the hatred of the world. (Notice the parallels in this section to Matthew's mission sermon.) The opposition between the world subject to Satan (1 Jn 5:19) and Jesus will continue between the world and Jesus' disciples. Since the works of the world are evil (Jn 7:7), the disciples cannot be followers of Jesus and partake in the world's works at the same time. The real cause of the world's hatred of Jesus is the world's (and its master's) hatred of God the Father. (Notice in v. 21 that the disciples will be persecuted "on account of my name"—a reference to the divine name "I am" which appears often in John.) The injustice of the world's hatred will call for the services of the Paraclete, the Spirit of true witness. The instruments of the Paraclete's testimony will be the disciples who were with Jesus from the time John the Baptist bore witness. Thus it is through the church that the Spirit will tell people about Jesus.

This warning about the world's persecution is precautionary. Beginning with the death of Stephen, the first martyr, love of God will be the mask of the world's hate. The expulsion

Marginal references: Jn 3:34-35; 18 — Jn 15; Mt 10 v. 18 = 22; 20a = 24-25; 20b = 23; 21 = 22; 26 = 19-20; 27 = 18; 19 — Jn 17:15-16; Acts 5:41; #3a. 21-23 — . 24-26 — . 27 — Acts 1:21-22; 1:8; 1 Jn 1:1-3; 4:13-14. 16:1 — . 2 — Acts 7:54-58.

83

17 **The Prayer of Jesus.** ¹When Jesus had said this, he raised his eyes to heaven and said, "Father, the hour has come. Give glory to your son, so that your son may glorify you, ²just as you gave him authority over all people, so that he may give eternal life to all you gave him. ³Now this is eternal life, that they should know you, the only true God, and the one whom you sent, Jesus Christ. ⁴I glorified you on earth by accomplishing the work that you gave me

from the synagogues is a specification of Jesus' anticipation of persecution made in light of the Johannine Community's harsh experience of Jewish rejection already alluded to in 9:23 and 12:42. Just as Jesus has an hour (an hour of glorification which involves suffering), so too the hour of his followers must come. **4** The disciples have been bidden to share in the Lord's blood both in the eucharistic sense and in the natural sense.

Ap 13:11-15

Jn 6:53

Part Three of the Last Discourse—17:1-26

The "Priestly Prayer" constituting this chapter is a unit in itself, the sublime conclusion of the Last Discourse. Here, more than ever, we cross the threshold of eternity. Although still in the world (v. 13), Jesus looks on his earthly ministry as a thing of the past (v. 4). In John we have seen very little of the prayer of Jesus; when he has prayed, it has been to teach his hearers about the source of his glory. Here we have the glorified high priest returning to his Father and, as a representative of humanity, presenting a great prayer of union. Drawing a parallel from liturgy, we have here the Preface to the historical and eternally valid offering of the cross. (The reader may find it interesting to search out echoes of that other prayer of Jesus in the Synoptics, the Our Father.)

Jn 11:41-42; 12:27-28

Heb 7:26-27; 9:24 1 Jn 2:1

Mt 6:9-13

All is consummated; prayer for glory—17:1-8

The opening words link this section to the rest of the discourse. As at the multiplication of the loaves, Jesus lifts up his eyes to heaven, seeking the source of his glory. We are in the context of John's "hour," so much so that Jesus can now be the **2** source of eternal life which is the fruit of his glorification. For only when Jesus is glorified is the glory of the Father fully **4** evident. The Son became man to reveal the Father whom no **3** one had even seen; only now is that task fully accomplished, for only now can people *know* the Father as he is reflected in his glorious Son. The Semitic use of "know" implies intimacy and union; here it is union with the source of life, the Father

Mk 6:41; Jn 6:5

Jn 7:38-39

Jn 1:18 1 Jn 5:20 #5

to do. [5]Now glorify me, Father, with you, with the glory that I had with you before the world began.

[6]"I revealed your name to those whom you gave me out of the world. They belonged to you, and you gave them to me, and they have kept your word. [7]Now they know that everything you gave me is from you, [8]because the words you gave to me I have given to them, and they accepted them and truly understood that I came from you, and they have believed that you sent me. [9]I pray for them. I do not pray for the world but for the ones you have given me, because they are yours, [10]and everything of mine is yours and everything of yours is mine, and I have been glorified in them. [11]And now I will no longer be in the world, but they are in the world, while I am coming to you. Holy Father, keep them in your name that you have given me, so that they may be one just as we are. [12]When I was with them I protected them in your name that you gave me, and I guarded them, and none of them was lost except the son of destruction, in order that the scripture might be fulfilled. [13]But now I am coming to you. I speak this in the world so that they may share my joy completely. [14]I gave them your word, and the world hated them, because they do not belong to the world any more than I belong to the world. [15]I do not ask that you take them out of the world but that you keep them from the evil one. [16]They do not belong to the world any more than I belong to the world. [17]Consecrate them

who speaks through the Word. Theology agrees fully with John's concept of eternal life when it tells us that heaven and the beatific vision consist in the intuitive knowledge of God, the completion of the imperfect knowledge begun here below.

5 With the accomplishment of the work of revealing the Father, the Son returns to the right hand of the Father. Actually as God, the Son had never left the Father; but now the human nature he assumed is to be glorified in the Father's presence.

6 Once again we note a Johannine reference to the divine
7-8 name ("I am"). Those who receive Jesus are the ones already chosen by the Father, another Johannine theme.

Margin references: 1 Jn 3:2; 1 Cor 13:12; Eph 1:20-22; Jn 1:18; 8:29

Cf. Jn 6:20; Jn 8:24, 28, 58; Jn 1:12-13; 6:65

Prayer for the disciples—17:9-19

These chosen believers, now the common property of the Father and the incarnate Son, are the first object of Jesus' prayer; he prays for their protection (verses 9-16) and their dedication (verses 17-19). What will become of them now that the
11 shepherd is leaving? On earth Jesus was able to protect them;
12 now he asks that protection be continued "in your name that you have given me" (for an example of the divine name exercising protection, see 18:6-9; also Acts 4:12). Judas, the only exception to this protection, was not the product of weakness on Jesus' part; rather he was part of the divine plan as witnessed in the Old Testament. The themes of the joy of the disciples and the hatred of the world that we saw in Part II now
13-14 recur. Here it is clearer that there is to be no withdrawal from
15-16,

Margin references: Jn 10:28-29; Mk 14:27; Lk 22:32

Jn 15:11, 18ff

in the truth. Your word is truth. ¹⁸As you sent me into the world, so I sent them into the world. ¹⁹And I consecrate myself for them, so that they also may be consecrated in truth.

²⁰"I pray not only for them, but also for those who will believe in me through their word, ²¹so that they may all be one, as you, Father, are in me and I in you, that they also may be in us, that the world may believe that you sent me. ²²And I have given them the glory you gave me, so that they may be one, as we are one, ²³I in them and you in me, that they may be brought to perfection as one, that the world may know that you sent me, and that you loved them even as you loved me. ²⁴Father, they are your gift to me. I wish that where I am they also may be with me, that they may see my glory that you gave me, because you loved me before the foundation of the world.

18   the struggle with the empire of Satan; the disciples are sent in frontal assault on the world to conquer it for Christ. In principle, Jesus has won the victory; but the working-out of that victory in time is the work of the disciples, the church. To
17,   strengthen them in their work, which is the continuation of
19   his own, Jesus consecrates himself, i.e., dedicates himself as a sacrifice, that from his consecration they may receive the necessary dedication and sanctification. These verses are a promise of a divine mission for the disciples, a mission that will be given them on Easter night after the sacrifice has been completed. The truth which is the seal of the sanctification of the disciples is the revelation made in Jesus and interpreted by the Spirit of truth. (A statement such as "Your word is truth"— notice also "word" in 17:6 and 14—combined with "I am the truth" may have formed the basis of John's description of Jesus as the Word in the Prologue.)

Margin references: Jn 16:33 / 1 Jn 5:4 / Eph 6:11-13 / Cf. Jn 10:36 / Eph 5:25-26 / Jn 20:21 / Jn 14:6

Prayer for those who believe through the disciples' word—17:20-26

As in 10:16, believers (evangelized by different disciples) are not one flock, but unity is prayed for. Vital contact with this future generation and all subsequent generations will not be
21-23 lost, for Jesus will dwell in them. The indwelling of Jesus, the Christian's earthly share in eternal life, provides the great bond of union connecting Christians of all times with the Father. Jesus' love for them is the same as his love for his immediate disciples: a love patterned on the eternal love of the Father for the Son. (So perfect is this love that it will force even the
24   world's recognition!) And they too shall have a share in the eternal glory of the Son.
25-26 With this cry of triumph as a close to his prayer, Jesus draws all of us into his embrace. The world has refused to hear his Father; but we who believe have known the Father, and thus

Margin references: Jn 20:29, 31 / Mt 28:20 / 1 Jn 1:3

Jh. 17:20-26

²⁵Righteous Father, the world also does not know you, but I know you, and they know that you sent me. ²⁶I made known to them your name and I will make it known, that the love with which you loved me may be in them and I in them."

18 **Jesus Arrested.** ¹When he had said this, Jesus went out with his disciples across the Kidron valley to where there was a garden, into which he and his disciples entered. ²Judas his betrayer also knew the place, because Jesus had often met there with his disciples. ³So Judas got a band of soldiers and guards from the chief priests and the Pharisees and went there with lanterns, torches, and

weapons. ⁴Jesus, knowing everything that was going to happen to him, went out and said to them, "Whom are you looking for?" ⁵They answered him, "Jesus the Nazorean." He said to them, "I AM." Judas his betrayer was also with them. ⁶When he said to them, "I AM," they turned away and fell to the ground. ⁷So he again asked them, "Whom are you looking for?" They said, "Jesus the Nazorean." ⁸Jesus answered, "I told you that I AM. So if you are looking for me, let these men go." ⁹This was to fulfill what he had said, "I have not lost any of those you gave me." ¹⁰Then Simon Peter, who had a sword, drew it, struck the high

have a share in his love and in his Son. Jesus had made his Father known; now he proceeds to the ultimate revelation of the cross, the resurrection, and the distribution of the Spirit. "I have made known to them your name, and I will make it known."

Section 2. Trial and Death (18:1–19:42)

In the garden—18:1-12

At the close of his Last Supper Discourse (perhaps continuing 14:31), Jesus leaves for the garden which Mark-Matthew call Gethsemane, across the winter-flowing wadi of the Kidron to the Mount of Olives. Jesus' agony at this site, described in the Synoptics, is absent from John, although details of it seem to appear elsewhere. John begins with Judas leading the arresting party to this place. The squad is sent by the Jewish authorities; but in John alone do Roman troops ("band" is "cohort") led by a Roman tribune appear (a detail which may well indicate Pilate's knowledge of the arrest). In this attempt of darkness to extinguish the light of the world, the ministers of darkness need lamps. Omitting the incident of Judas' kiss, John has Jesus taking the initiative, ever the master of his destiny. As he utters the divine name, "I am (he)," the forces of darkness are helpless, struck with fear as Moses was at Sinai. Ever careful of those the Father has given him, Jesus uses his power to protect his disciples. The story of the servant's ear is told with more detail than in the Synoptics, for only John names the

Mk 14:32ff

#8a

Jn 12:27-29; 14:31; 18:11
Lk 22:39

Jn 12:35

Jn 10:18
Ex 3:6, 14

Lk 22:50-51;
Mk 14:47

2
3, 12
4-5
6-7
8-9
10-11

priest's slave, and cut off his right ear. The slave's name was Malchus. ¹¹Jesus said to Peter, "Put your sword into its scabbard. Shall I not drink the cup that the Father gave me?"

¹²So the band of soldiers, the tribune, and the Jewish guards seized Jesus, bound him, ¹³and brought him to Annas first. He was the father-in-law of Caiaphas, who was high priest that year. ¹⁴It was Caiaphas who had counseled the Jews that it was better that one man should die rather than the people.

Peter's First Denial. ¹⁵Simon Peter and another disciple followed Jesus. Now the other disciple was known to the high priest, and he entered the courtyard of the high priest with Jesus. ¹⁶But Peter stood at the gate outside. So the other disciple, the acquaintance of the high priest, went out and spoke to the gatekeeper and brought Peter in. ¹⁷Then the maid who was the gatekeeper said to Peter, "You are not one of this man's disciples, are you?" He said, "I am not." ¹⁸Now the slaves and the guards were standing around a charcoal fire that they had made, because it was cold, and were warming themselves. Peter was also standing there keeping warm.

The Inquiry before Annas. ¹⁹The high priest questioned Jesus about his disciples

characters, Peter and Malchus. The saying about the cup is another detail from the absent agony scene. `Mk 14:36`

Inquiry before Annas—18:13-14, 19-24

Mark-Matthew narrate a Sanhedrin night trial (Mt: before Caiaphas); Luke reports a similar scene in the morning (and no night trial). Mark-Matthew merely mention a morning session of the Sanhedrin. Since a formal session of the Sanhedrin at night would have been irregular, these differing accounts may represent an oversimplification of a complex of actions: (a) an unofficial night inquiry by the high priest Annas (of whose part only John knows) where Jesus was ill treated and during which Peter denied him; (b) in the morning a Sanhedrin hearing before Caiaphas with the definitive resolve to have Jesus executed by the Romans. John gives only the outline, the Synoptics give details. `Mk 14:53-65; Lk 22:66-71` `Mk 15:1` `Lk 22:54-65; Mk 14:65-72` `Jn 18:24, 28; Lk 22:66-71; Mk 14:55-64`

13-14 Annas was the patriarch in a family of high priests. High priest himself in A.D. 6–15, he had five sons, a grandson and a son-in-law (Caiaphas) who served as high priests. The house of Annas is notorious in rabbinic literature for avarice and corruption. Caiaphas, who held office from A.D. 18 to 36, fell from power as soon as Pontius Pilate was dismissed, and we may suspect some collusion between the two. The tradition that a high priest (whom John identifies as Annas) was involved in the night session may have prompted Matthew's identification of this high priest as Caiaphas, the actually reigning high priest. `Lk 3:2; Acts 4:6` `Mt 26:57`

19 The night questioning in John, which bears no similarity to the Synoptic trial, concerns Jesus' teaching (How did he teach,

and about his doctrine. ²⁰Jesus answered him, "I have spoken publicly to the world. I have always taught in a synagogue or in the temple area where all the Jews gather, and in secret I have said nothing. ²¹Why ask me? Ask those who heard me what I said to them. They know what I said." ²²When he had said this, one of the temple guards standing there struck Jesus and said, "Is this the way you answer the high priest?" ²³Jesus answered him, "If I have spoken wrongly, testify to the wrong; but if I have spoken rightly,

why do you strike me?" ²⁴Then Annas sent him bound to Caiaphas the high priest.

Peter Denies Jesus Again. ²⁵Now Simon Peter was standing there keeping warm. And they said to him, "You are not one of his disciples, are you?" He denied it and said, "I am not." ²⁶One of the slaves of the high priest, a relative of the one whose ear Peter had cut off, said, "Didn't I see you in the garden with him?" ²⁷Again Peter denied it. And immediately the cock crowed.

never being formally trained?) and his disciples (Was there danger of messianic uprising?). The answer of Jesus (which appears in the Synoptic garden scene—Mk 14:49) stresses the public nature of his ministry: nothing of real import to his inquirers has been hidden. At this informal inquiry, the abuse of the witness seems more in place than at the Sanhedrin trial (where the Synoptic tradition, having details on only one trial, places it). John omits the details of the Sanhedrin trial about messiahship (the Synoptic trial), but, true to his literary style, seems to mention incidents from it elsewhere in the Gospel.

20
21
22-23
24

#8a
Mk 14:58
= Jn 2:19;
Lk 22:67-
68 = Jn
10:24-25;
Lk 22:70 =
Jn 10:36;
19:7; Mk
14:62 = Jn
1:51; Mk
14:64 =
Jn 11:53

Peter's denial—18:15-18, 25-27

To show that Peter's denials were contemporary with the night inquiry (all four Gospels have the denials at night), John puts the first denial before the account of the inquiry, and the second and third after it. The exact identity of the three persons who ask the questions of Peter varies among the Gospels (as we would expect in oral tradition), but the basic import of the story remains the same—an uncomplimentary tribute to Peter's importance. John's most noteworthy contribution is that "the other disciple" who was known to the high priest gained entrance for Peter. This is the first use of the term "the other disciple"; Jn 20:2 identifies him with "the disciple whom Jesus loved." Perhaps "the other disciple" was the disciple's own self-description, and the second, more laudatory title was used of him by his own disciples. In any case, the connection with Peter is typical of this disciple. We do not know in what capacity he "was known to the high priest," but this information probably gave rise to the second-century tradition that John (thought to be the disciple) was a priest.

15-16

Jn 13:23-
24; 20:2-3;
21:7,
20-21

The Trial before Pilate. [28]Then they brought Jesus from Caiaphas to the praetorium. It was morning. And they themselves did not enter the praetorium, in order not to be defiled so that they could eat the Passover. [29]So Pilate came out to them and said, "What charge do you bring [against] this man?" [30]They answered and said to him, "If he were not a criminal, we would not have handed him over to you." [31]At this, Pilate said to them, "Take him yourselves, and judge him according to your law." The Jews answered him, "We do not have the right to execute anyone," [32]in order that the word of Jesus might be fulfilled that he

The trial before Pilate—18:28–19:16

Fr. Boismard has observed that this trial is arranged in seven scenes, alternating outside (O) and inside (I) the praetorium:

(1) O—Jews demand death: 18:28-32

(2) I—Pilate questions Jesus —kingship: 18:33-38a

(3) O—Jesus innocent: 18:38b-40

(4) I—Mocking of Jesus: 19:1-3

(5) O—Jesus innocent: 19:4-8

(6) I—Pilate questions Jesus —power: 19:9-12a

(7) O—Jews obtain death: 19:12b-16

While the Synoptics have elements of scenes 2, 3, 4, 5, 7, they do not have the alternation of scene nor such a dramatic arrangement. By having Pilate shuttle between the Jews outside and Jesus inside, John puts the indecisive on trial for failing to listen to the truth.

Scene One—18:28-32

The time and scene directions are precise: it is early Friday morning (Passover will begin at sunset); we are outside the praetorium (entering a Gentile's house might render the priests ritually impure). Only the Fourth Gospel explains the reason for coming to Pilate at all, viz., the Romans have deprived the Jews of the power to execute. And by insisting that the Jews present a charge, Pilate forces them to admit they want execution by crucifixion, a Roman punishment.

29-31

32

Scene Two—18:33-38a

As in Mark-Matthew, Pilate seems to have previous knowledge of the allegation against Jesus; in Luke he is informed of the accusations. As far as the Romans are concerned, the case will center on the political charge, lèse majesté against Rome, and not any charge of blasphemy. In the Synoptics, Jesus answers the question on kingship with a qualified, "You have said so," which implies: "What you have said is correct, but I

Mk 15:2

Lk 23:2

Jn 19:13-14, 19

Mk 15:2

said indicating the kind of death he would die. ³³So Pilate went back into the praetorium and summoned Jesus and said to him, "Are you the King of the Jews?" ³⁴Jesus answered, "Do you say this on your own or have others told you about me?" ³⁵Pilate answered, "I am not a Jew, am I? Your own nation and the chief priests handed you over to me. What have you done?" ³⁶Jesus answered, "My kingdom does not belong to this world. If my kingdom did belong to this world, my attendants [would] be fighting to keep me from being handed over to the Jews. But as it is, my kingdom is not here." ³⁷So Pilate said to him, "Then you are a king?" Jesus answered, "You say I am a king. For this I was born and for this I came into the world, to testify to the truth. Everyone who belongs to the truth listens to my voice." ³⁸Pilate said to him, "What is truth?"

When he had said this, he again went out to the Jews and said to them, "I find no guilt in him. ³⁹But you have a custom that I release one prisoner to you at Passover. Do you want me to release to you the King of the Jews?" ⁴⁰They cried out again, "Not this one but Barabbas!" Now Barabbas was a revolutionary.

19 ¹Then Pilate took Jesus and had him scourged. ²And the soldiers wove a crown out of thorns and placed it on his head, and clothed him in a purple cloak, ³and they came to him and said, "Hail, King of the Jews!" And they struck

34-35 would not give it the connotation you intend." John clarifies this ambiguity by reporting Jesus' careful explanation of his kingship. There is a distinction between the Gentile political understanding of the kingship of the Jews and the Jewish religious understanding whereby God is king of Israel. Jesus ex- **36** plains to Pilate that his kingdom is not a political one (the statement that otherwise he would have aid in protecting it has a **37** parallel verse in the Synoptic garden scene). The purpose of the incarnation is better understood in terms of testifying to the **38a** truth—a testimony that constitutes judgment for Pilate who seeks to avoid it. *Ex 15:18; Is 33:22; Ps 95:3* *Mt 26:53*

Scene Three—18:38b-40

As in Luke, Pilate's first proclamation of "not guilty" follows the interrogation on kingship. The Barabbas scene is familiar from the Synoptics. John identifies Barabbas as a bandit (brigand or guerrilla warrior), matching the Synoptic information that he was a revolutionary. There is little evidence for a custom of releasing such a criminal. *Lk 23:4 Mk 15:7; Lk 23:19*

Scene Four—19:1-3

John gives the scourging and mocking scene a dramatically central place in the trial. Perhaps historically the two actions were separated. Luke has a mocking before Herod (only Luke reports Herod's questioning). Mark-Matthew have the scourging at the end of Pilate's trial; it usually formed a part of the crucifixion punishment in order to weaken the prisoner. We may see *Lk 23:11* *Mk 15:15-20*

him repeatedly. ⁴Once more Pilate went out and said to them, "Look, I am bringing him out to you, so that you may know that I find no guilt in him." ⁵So Jesus came out, wearing the crown of thorns and the purple cloak. And he said to them, "Behold, the man!" ⁶When the chief priests and the guards saw him they cried out, "Crucify him, crucify him!" Pilate said to them, "Take him yourselves and crucify him. I find no guilt in him." ⁷The Jews answered, "We have a law, and according to that law he ought to die, because he made himself the Son of God." ⁸Now when Pilate heard this statement, he became even more afraid, ⁹and went back into the praetorium and said to Jesus, "Where are you from?" Jesus did not answer him. ¹⁰So Pilate said to him, "Do you not speak to me? Do you not know that I have power to release you and I have power to crucify you?" ¹¹Jesus answered [him], "You would have no power over me if it had not been given to you from above. For this reason the one who handed me over to you has the greater sin." ¹²Consequently, Pilate tried to release him; but the Jews cried out, "If you release him, you are not a Friend of Caesar. Everyone who makes himself a king opposes Caesar."

¹³When Pilate heard these words he brought Jesus out and seated him on the judge's bench in the place called Stone

3   irony in the Gentiles' acclaiming Jesus as king; long before the   #2
account was written they would do this without mockery.

Scene Five—19:4-8

Pilate's second "not guilty," both in John and Luke; follows   Lk 23:14
5   the mocking. In the hope of gaining sympathy, Pilate presents
7   the Man of Sorrows. The Jews reject him, not as man, but
6   because he has made himself Son of God. To their double cry   Is 53:2-3
for crucifixion, Pilate returns his third "not guilty" in John and   Lk
22:70-71
Luke. Openly, now, the real issue is religious, not political.   Lk 23:22

Scene Six—19:9-12a

Frightened by this talk about Son of God, Pilate interrogates
Jesus on his origin. (Perhaps Luke's interchange about Jesus'   Lk 23:6
origin in Galilee is related to this.) Certain to be misunderstood,
10-11 Jesus is silent. Before Pilate's claim of power, Jesus shows he   Mk 15:5
is still master; for Pilate's power depends on the Father's will.
The ultimate iniquity is not Pilate's but the real traitor's—   Jn 13:2
Satan's. Notice how Jesus puts Pilate on the defensive.

Scene Seven—19:12b-16

In the last scene, John alone shows clearly why Pilate really   Mk 15:15
yielded, viz., the threat of Caesar. (The praetorium is the place
where a Roman praetor rendered judgment. Of the two possible sites for the praetorium in Jerusalem, Herod's palace in the west is more plausible than the fortress Antonia in the east.
13-14 "Lithostrotos" implies a large stone pavement, but the pave-

Pavement, in Hebrew, Gabbatha. [14]It was preparation day for Passover, and it was about noon. And he said to the Jews, "Behold, your king!" [15]They cried out, "Take him away, take him away! Crucify him!" Pilate said to them, "Shall I crucify your king?" The chief priests answered, "We have no king but Caesar." [16]Then he handed him over to them to be crucified.

The Crucifixion of Jesus. So they took Jesus, [17]and carrying the cross himself he went out to what is called the Place of the Skull, in Hebrew, Golgotha. [18]There they crucified him, and with him two others, one on either side, with Jesus in the middle. [19]Pilate also had an inscription written and put on the cross. It read, "Jesus the Nazorean, the King of the Jews." [20]Now many of the Jews read this inscription, because the place where Jesus was crucified was near the city; and it was written in Hebrew, Latin, and Greek. [21]So the chief priests of the Jews said to Pilate, "Do not write 'The King of the Jews,' but that he said, 'I am the King of the Jews.'" [22]Pilate answered, "What I have written, I have written."

[23]When the soldiers had crucified Jesus, they took his clothes and divided them into four shares, a share for each soldier.

ment found at Antonia dates from a century after Jesus.) Mounting his judgment-seat, as was necessary for a capital sentence, Pilate (here with deep Johannine irony) proclaims the kingship of Jesus. In their rejection of Jesus, the people who once claimed God as their king are forced to accept Caesar as their king. The meaning of the trial is now clear; the presence of Jesus has provoked a judgment whereby the Chosen People have abandoned their birthright. To emphasize the really guilty, John says that Pilate handed Jesus over "to them," i.e., to the chief priests, to be crucified (although, obviously, it was the Roman soldiers who took charge). The time of this fatal hour in Israel's history is noon (v. 14), the very moment when the priests have begun the slaughter of the paschal lambs in the Temple.

Margin references: Mt 27:19; #2; 15 — Jg 8:23; Zeph 3:15; Jn 3:19; 16 — Mk 15:16; Jn 1:29; #4

Jesus is put to death—19:17-37

Jesus goes to death bearing his cross, once again in full charge of his destiny. (John omits many of the Synoptic details of the crucifixion, e.g., Simon of Cyrene, the wailing women, the drugged potion, the raillery of the onlookers, the darkness, the admiring centurion, the tearing of the Temple veil. As usual, emphasis centers on incidents with theological import.) The plaque announcing the crime of the accused is mentioned in all four Gospels, but in four different wordings (an interesting example of how oral tradition preserved the substance, but not the exact details). The solemn form in John is a trilingual proclamation. Pilate's defiant insistence that its first wording remain intact indicates ironically that the Gentiles will ultimately uphold the kingship of Christ.

Margin references: 19-20 — Mk 15:26; Mt 27:37; Lk 23:38; 21-22 — #2

They also took his tunic, but the tunic was seamless, woven in one piece from the top down. [24]So they said to one another, "Let's not tear it, but cast lots for it to see whose it will be," in order that the passage of scripture might be fulfilled [that says]:

"They divided my garments among them,
and for my vesture they cast lots."

This is what the soldiers did. [25]Standing by the cross of Jesus were his mother and his mother's sister, Mary the wife of Clo-pas, and Mary of Magdala. [26]When Jesus saw his mother and the disciple there whom he loved, he said to his mother, "Woman, behold, your son." [27]Then he said to the disciple, "Behold, your mother." And from that hour the disciple took her into his home.

[28]After this, aware that everything was now finished, in order that the scripture might be fulfilled, Jesus said, "I thirst." [29]There was a vessel filled with common wine. So they put a sponge soaked in wine on a sprig of hyssop and put it up

---

23-24   In the stripping incident, John sees the same prophecy fulfilled which the Synoptics tacitly cite (from Ps 22, which begins, "My God, my God, why have you forsaken me?"). Yet John alone stresses the seamless tunic woven in one piece (a garment something like a priest's alb). Josephus gives a very similar description of the high priest's robe, and John may wish to show that Jesus died, not only as a king, but likewise as a priest. Or else he is symbolically stressing Christian unity. *(Mk 15:24; Ps 22:19; Mk 15:34; Ant III, 7, 4; Jn 10:16; 17:21)*

25   The Synoptics report a group of women standing afar off: (a) Mary Magdalene; (b) Mary, mother of James and Joseph (or Joses); (c) Salome, probably wife of Zebedee and mother of James and John. The Fourth Gospel reports the beloved disciple and four women standing at the foot of the cross: (a) the mother of Jesus; (b) her unnamed sister (Salome?—this would make Zebedee's sons cousins of Jesus); (c) Mary (wife?) of Clopas; (d) Mary Magdalene. Actually (b) and (c) can be read in apposition, making Mary of Clopas the sister of Jesus' mother, but it is unlikely to have two sisters with the same name. *(Mk 15:40; Mt 27:56; Mt 13:55; Mk 6:3)*

26-27   For the significance of the mother of Jesus and the beloved disciple (neither of whom are ever named), we refer back to Cana. The mother whose family request was rebuked there is now given the role of the mother of the ideal disciples— compare Mk 3:31-35 on the priority of discipleship over family demands. *(Jn 2:4)*

28   **29**   With this commission to his mother, Jesus has finished the work he came to do. In the incident of the wine, Mark-Matthew more appropriately mention a reed as the instrument for elevating the sponge to Jesus' mouth. John's hyssop, a fern-like plant, is strange until we remember that hyssop dipped in the blood of the *paschal lamb* was used to smear doorposts *(Jn 17:4; Mk 15:36; Ex 12:22)*

to his mouth. ³⁰When Jesus had taken the wine, he said, "It is finished." And bowing his head, he handed over the spirit.

The Blood and Water. ³¹Now since it was preparation day, in order that the bodies might not remain on the cross on the sabbath, for the sabbath day of that week was a solemn one, the Jews asked Pilate that their legs be broken and they be taken down. ³²So the soldiers came and broke the legs of the first and then of the other one who was crucified with Jesus. ³³But when they came to Jesus and saw that he was already dead, they did not break his legs, ³⁴but one soldier thrust his lance into his side, and immediately blood and water flowed out. ³⁵An eyewitness has testified, and his testimony is true; he knows that he is speaking the truth, so that you also may [come to] believe. ³⁶For this happened so that the scripture passage might be fulfilled:

as a sign of God's protection in the Jewish Passover reenactment of the exodus.

30   Matthew and Luke tell how Jesus yielded up his spirit (in the sense of breath of life) or how he entrusted his spirit to the Father. John seems to imply a deeper meaning, for he says literally: "He handed over the spirit." Jesus had promised the communication of the Spirit when he would be glorified, 31-34 and here the Spirit is handed over to the beloved disciple. In the same vein, the Fourth Gospel mentions an incident unknown to the Synoptic tradition, an incident so important that the disciple testifies to it (v. 35): the piercing of the side of Jesus from which there came blood and water. In his life Jesus had spoken of the water of life that he would give; he had said of himself: "From within him there shall flow rivers of living water." Now that he is glorified, raised up on the cross, the water that flows from within him, permeated with the blood of his self-giving, is truly the water of life bringing salvation to people. The Spirit and the living water—these are the means for the rebirth by water and the Spirit that had been promised Nicodemus. Small wonder that St. Augustine and others see in the water and the blood the fundamental Christian sacraments of baptism and the eucharist flowing from Jesus' redemptive death—indeed, the birth of the church from the side of Jesus (the new Eve from the side of the new Adam?).

Pressing on, John sees two Old Testament citations fulfilled in the piercing of Jesus. The text on not breaking a bone is again from the ritual of the *paschal lamb* (also, perhaps, the desire to remove Jesus' body from the cross the *same day* in v. 31). This text also appears in a psalm which describes a suffering, righteous man. Thus at the end of Jesus' life the beloved disciple (v. 35) bears witness to him as paschal Lamb and Suffering Servant, the same witness given by John the Baptist at

Mt 27:50;
Lk 23:46

#3a

Jn 7:39

Jn 4:10
Jn 7:38

1 Jn 5:8

Jn 3:5;
1:33

Gn
2:21-23

Ex 12:46

Ex 12:10
#3b
Ps 34:21
Cf. Jn
1:29
#4

"Not a bone of it will be broken." ³⁷And again another passage says:
"They will look upon him whom they have pierced."

The Burial of Jesus. ³⁸After this, Joseph of Arimathea, secretly a disciple of Jesus for fear of the Jews, asked Pilate if he could remove the body of Jesus. And Pilate permitted it. So he came and took his body. ³⁹Nicodemus, the one who had first come to him at night, also came bringing a mixture of myrrh and aloes weighing about one hundred pounds. ⁴⁰They took the body of Jesus and bound it with burial cloths along with the spices, according to the Jewish burial custom. ⁴¹Now in the place where he had been crucified there was a garden, and in the garden a new tomb, in which no one had yet been buried. ⁴²So they laid Jesus there because of the Jewish preparation day; for the tomb was close by.

20 **The Empty Tomb.** ¹On the first day of the week, Mary of Magdala came to the tomb early in the morning, while it was still dark, and saw the stone removed from the tomb. ²So she ran and went to Simon Peter and to the other dis-

---

37 the beginning. The second citation, referring in the Old Testament to Israel's rejection of God, promises in its original context the pouring forth of God's spirit and the opening of a fountain of cleansing for Jerusalem. Thus, this passage, too, echoes John the Baptist's description of Jesus' mission.

Za 12:10b
Za 12:10a; 13:1

Jn 1:33

The burial of Jesus—19:38-42

All the Gospels mention the role of Joseph of Arimathea. One of the wealthy lay members of the Sanhedrin ("elders"), he
39 buries Jesus in a new tomb. Only John mentions another Sanhedrin member, the Pharisee Nicodemus, who contributes an
40 immense amount of embalming spices. That Jesus was thus embalmed with spices before burial (without a hint that the process was incomplete) is not easily reconciled with the information in Mark and Luke (but not Matthew) that on Easter morning the women came with spices to the tomb. In any case, the brave action of the hitherto timid Joseph and Nicodemus seems to indicate that Jesus, raised up, has begun drawing people unto himself.

Mk 15:43

Mk 16:1;
Lk 24:1;
Mt 28:1
Jn 12:32

Section 3. The Resurrection Appearances in Jerusalem (20:1-31)

The three Synoptic Gospels, the Marcan Appendix (Mk 16:9ff), and 1 Cor 15:4-7 give us five accounts of resurrection appearances that should be carefully studied in relation to the Fourth Gospel. The differing details clearly rule out any organized attempt at inventing the incidents involved. Different apologetic and doctrinal interest in these various compositions seems to guide the choice of appearances and details. John's Jerusalem appearances may be divided as follows:

ciple whom Jesus loved, and told them, "They have taken the Lord from the tomb, and we don't know where they put him." ³So Peter and the other disciple went out and came to the tomb. ⁴They both ran, but the other disciple ran faster than Peter and arrived at the tomb first; ⁵he bent down and saw the burial cloths there, but did not go in. ⁶When Simon Peter arrived after him, he went into the tomb and saw the burial cloths there, ⁷and the cloth that had covered his head, not with the burial cloths but rolled up in a separate place. ⁸Then the other disciple also went in, the one who had arrived at the tomb first, and he saw and believed. ⁹For they did not yet understand the scripture that he had to rise from the dead. ¹⁰Then the disciples returned home.

The Appearance to Mary of Magdala. ¹¹But Mary stayed outside the tomb weeping. And as she wept, she bent over into

Scene One: The Tomb (20:1-18)	(a) Peter and beloved disciple; latter believes; Mary absent
	(b) Mary, in sorrow, led to belief
Scene Two: Upper Room (20:19-31)	(a) Disciples believe; Thomas absent
	(b) Thomas, doubting, led to belief

Scene One: the two disciples—20:1-10

On Sunday morning, Mary Magdalene (with companions, as the "we" of v. 2 shows), finding the tomb empty and suspect-
3-4 ing tomb robbery, hastens to inform Peter and "the other disciple" who is identified also as the one "whom Jesus loved." In the resurrection accounts, Peter has a special place among the
5-7 disciples. John is very careful about the state of the linen cloths (bands?) used to wrap the corpse, and the separate piece for the head. Their position may have outlined the original position of Jesus' body which passed through them, leaving them
8 where they were. The sight was enough to warrant belief in the resurrection on the disciple's part but seemingly not on Peter's. (First to believe in the risen Jesus is "the other disciple.") An aside tells us that the full outpouring of the Spirit,
9 the interpreter of Scripture, had not yet occurred.

Mk 16:1; Lk 24:10

Mk 16:17; Lk 24:34; 1 Cor 15:5

Jn 14:26; Lk 24:45

Scene One: Mary Magdalene—20:11-18

Only John narrates the appearance to Mary after the disciples leave, although the Synoptics seem to give some of its details in their account of Mary's first (and, for them, only) visit to the tomb. In the tomb she sees two angels (Luke: two men standing inside; Mark: a young man sitting inside; Matthew: an angel sitting outside—the variants of oral tradition). The

Mt 28:8-10

Lk 24:4; Mk 16:5

Mt 28:2

the tomb [12]and saw two angels in white sitting there, one at the head and one at the feet where the body of Jesus had been. [13]And they said to her, "Woman, why are you weeping?" She said to them, "They have taken my Lord, and I don't know where they laid him." [14]When she had said this, she turned around and saw Jesus there, but did not know it was Jesus. [15]Jesus said to her, "Woman, why are you weeping? Whom are you looking for?" She thought it was the gardener and said to him, "Sir, if you carried him away, tell me where you laid him, and I will take him." [16]Jesus said to her, "Mary!" She turned and said to him in Hebrew, "Rabbouni," which means Teacher. [17]Jesus said to her, "Stop holding on to me, for I have not yet ascended to the Father. But go to my brothers and tell them, 'I am going to my Father and your Father, to my God and your God.' " [18]Mary of Magdala went and announced to the disciples, "I have seen the Lord," and what he told her.

Appearance to the Disciples. [19]On the evening of that first day of the week, when the doors were locked, where the disciples were, for fear of the Jews, Jesus

13 view of the interior of the tomb produced faith in the disciple;
    Mary, however, still thinks only of tomb robbery. Jesus him-
14 self stands before her, and she fails to recognize him. (There   Lk 24:16;
    seems to be something strange about the appearance of the   Mk 16:12;
                                                                            Jn 21:4
16 risen Lord.) It takes the shepherd's voice to bring her to recog-   Jn 10:3-4
    nition. She seems to have attempted to grasp her beloved
17 rabbi ("Rabboni" is a caritative), but Jesus tells her not to hold
    him back, for he is about to ascend to his Father. He calls the
    disciples "my brothers" and speaks of "my Father and your
    Father" (= my Father who is now to be your Father), for the   Ruth
    ascension will enable Jesus to give that Spirit which begets the   1:16
    disciples anew (see 3:15), thus making God their Father.

    When we think of the ascension, we generally think of
    Luke's account of Jesus' levitation forty days after Easter. Yet   Acts 1:3, 9
    this is really no more than his visible departure from the world,
    and the official end of his post-resurrection appearances be-
    fore the visible mission of the Spirit on Pentecost. The theo-
    logical ascension, the glorification of Jesus' humanity in his   Rom 1:4
    Father's presence, was something invisible, and the inseparable
    completion of the resurrection. John makes clear that the ele-
    vation of Jesus which effected human salvation involves the   Jn 3;14-
    chain of crucifixion, resurrection, and ascension; these consti-   15; 12:32
    tute his ascent to his Father, reversing the incarnation process   Jn 3:13
    by which he descended to earth. John's account of the appear-
    ance to Mary seems designed to bring out the immediate con-
    nection between resurrection and ascension; for by Easter night
    and the first appearance to the apostles, Jesus' actions and state-
    ments already imply complete glorification, including ascen-
    sion. This is also true of his post-resurrection statements in the   Mt 28:18;
    Synoptic Gospels.   Lk 24:26

came and stood in their midst and said to them, "Peace be with you." [20]When he had said this, he showed them his hands and his side. The disciples rejoiced when they saw the Lord. [21][Jesus] said to them again, "Peace be with you. As the Father has sent me, so I send you." [22]And when he had said this, he breathed on them and said to them, "Receive the holy Spirit. [23]Whose sins you forgive are forgiven them, and whose sins you retain are retained."

Thomas. [24]Thomas, called Didymus, one of the Twelve, was not with them when Jesus came. [25]So the other disciples said to him, "We have seen the Lord." But he said to them, "Unless I see the mark of the nails in his hands and put my finger into the nailmarks and put my hand into his side, I will not believe." [26]Now

Scene Two: the disciples—20:19-23

Mary had brought the news of the resurrection to the disciples (the Synoptics indicate that she was met with disbelief). Now Jesus himself appears through shut doors on Sunday night (notice the importance of *Sunday* after the resurrection). John 19-20 records no rebuke or dismay, only the granting of the peace and joy that had been promised. (This post-resurrection account in John and Luke is our source for the knowledge that Jesus' hands and feet were nailed to the cross.) Jesus now 21-22 commissions his disciples formally and bestows the consecration of which he had spoken. He breathes on them as God had breathed (same Greek word) on Adam when infusing in him the spirit of life: Jesus is re-creating them with the Holy Spirit.

Once again we usually think of the Holy Spirit being given on Pentecost, but that is the official and public descent of the Spirit for directing the church's mission in the world. For John the gift of the Spirit, which of its nature is invisible, flows from the glorification of Jesus, his return to his Father. That a real gift of the Spirit is involved here on Easter night was made 23 clear at the Second Council of Constantinople. It is a gift that has relationship to the forgiveness of sins. A parallel text in Luke indicates that the immediate object may be the remission of sins in connection with conversion and baptism; but the Council of Trent has defined that the remission of sins committed after baptism through the sacrament of penance is (also) to be included.

Mk 16:9-11; Lk 24:22-25

Mk 16:14; Lk 24:37

Jn 14:27; 16:20-22

Lk 24:39

Jn 17:18-19

Gn 2:7

Acts 2

Jn 7:39

DBS 434

Lk 24:47

DBS 1703

1 Jn 1:7-9; 5:16-17

Scene Two: Thomas—20:24-31

John alone relates the incident of Thomas (about whom only 25 the Fourth Gospel contains information). Thomas demands physical proof of the resurrection, and thus renders the service of refuting any explanation of the resurrection appearances

Mk 3:18

Jn 11:16; 14:5

a week later his disciples were again inside and Thomas was with them. Jesus came, although the doors were locked, and stood in their midst and said, "Peace be with you." [27]Then he said to Thomas, "Put your finger here and see my hands, and bring your hand and put it into my side, and do not be unbelieving, but believe." [28]Thomas answered and said to him, "My Lord and my God!" [29]Jesus said to him, "Have you come to believe because you have seen me? Blessed are those who have not seen and have believed."

Conclusion. [30]Now Jesus did many other signs in the presence of [his] disciples that are not written in this book. [31]But these are written that you may [come to] believe that Jesus is the Messiah, the Son of God, and that through this belief you may have life in his name.

IV: EPILOGUE
THE RESURRECTION APPEARANCE IN GALILEE

21 **The Appearance to the Seven Disciples.** [1]After this, Jesus revealed himself again to his disciples at the Sea

26   as auto-suggestion or hallucination. Accordingly, on another *Sunday*, Jesus again appears through shut doors to the com-
27-28 plete number of disciples. The proof Thomas demanded is offered; but, seemingly without putting it to the test, Thomas confesses Jesus in the very words used by the Psalmist for Yahweh. In chapter one the disciples had given Jesus a series of titles indicating a gradually increasing knowledge of him; here Thomas gives the final title, the definitive one: Jesus is LORD GOD.

    On this triumphant and absolute affirmation of Jesus' divinity, the Gospel ends. At the beginning John told us *the Word*
29 *was God.* Now he repeats it at the end and blesses those who
30-31 accept it on faith, i.e., true Christians of all time. The purpose of the Gospel has been successfully accomplished: selected events have shown the divinity of Jesus so that, believing, the readers may have life through him.

Margin notes: 1 Cor 15:5? | Ps 35:23 Cf. Jn 1:43-45 | Jn 1:1 #4 1 Jn 4:15

EPILOGUE: APPEARANCES IN GALILEE

Jn 21:1-25

    Plausibly the Fourth Gospel once ended with c. 20. The supplementary c. 21 shows Johannine characteristics (e.g., Nathanael, Cana, beloved disciple), and so it probably represents another collection of early appearance stories which the final redactor found in the tradition and added to the work of the evangelist. (Clearly the sayings in 21:18, 22 were old enough to require explanation by the writer.) The presence of c. 21 in the early manuscripts (unlike the adulteress story) indicates that it was added before the Gospel was published.

Margin notes: Cf. p. 11 | Cf. Jn 7:53

of Tiberias. He revealed himself in this way. [2]Together were Simon Peter, Thomas called Didymus, Nathanael from Cana in Galilee, Zebedee's sons, and two others of his disciples. [3]Simon Peter said to them, "I am going fishing." They said to him, "We also will come with you." So they went out and got into the boat, but that night they caught nothing. [4]When it was already dawn, Jesus was standing on the shore; but the disciples did not realize that it was Jesus. [5]Jesus said to them, "Children, have you caught anything to eat?" They answered him, "No." [6]So he said to them, "Cast the net over the right side of the boat and you will find something." So they cast it, and were not able to pull it in because of the number of fish. [7]So the disciple whom Jesus loved said to Peter, "It is the Lord." When Simon Peter heard that it was the Lord, he tucked in his garment, for he was lightly clad, and jumped into the sea. [8]The other disciples came in the boat, for they were not far from shore, only about a hundred yards, dragging the net with the fish. [9]When they climbed out on shore, they saw a charcoal fire with fish on it and bread. [10]Jesus said to them, "Bring some of the fish you just caught."

Apart from two obvious editorial attempts to connect c. 21 with c. 20 (the "again" of v. 1 is textually doubtful), the resurrection appearances of c. 21 are autonomous, and seem to represent a Galilee tradition independent of the tradition of the Jerusalem appearances. Remember that basically Matthew and Mark proper (as distinct from the Marcan appendix: Mk 16:9-20) represent a tradition of Galilean appearances, while Luke and Jn 20 narrate only Jerusalem appearances.

Jn 21:1, 14

Mk 16:7;
Mt 28:10
Lk 24;
Acts 13:31

The fishermen—21:1-14

There seems to be a series of at least three separate scenes in c. 21 connected by tenuous (and perhaps editorial) threads.

2 The first pictures seven disciples fishing on the Lake of Galilee. The mention of the sons of Zebedee is extraordinary and unique in John; the two unnamed disciples are much more Johannine. (Perhaps "sons of Zebedee" is a gloss identifying the two "other disciples"; and thus there were only five.) V. 7 mentions the

Jn 1:35

3-4 beloved disciple. After the profitless night, Jesus appears and is not recognized. As mentioned, this is not extraordinary; yet if we connect this narrative to c. 20, the disciples had already

6 had two chances to examine him very closely! Thanks to the stranger's directions, there is a miraculous draught of fishes.

7 The disciple recognizes Jesus first with his usual "one-upmanship" over Peter; but Peter, with his penchant for jump-

9 ing from boats, is the first ashore. The presence of prepared fish and bread is curious, since Jesus had just asked them for fish (v. 5); but then an aura of mystery does surround these preternatural appearances.

Mt
14:28-31

11 The exact counting of the fish caught, 153, is probably sym-

¹¹So Simon Peter went over and dragged the net ashore full of one hundred fifty-three large fish. Even though there were so many, the net was not torn. ¹²Jesus said to them, "Come, have breakfast." And none of the disciples dared to ask him, "Who are you?" because they realized it was the Lord. ¹³Jesus came over and took the bread and gave it to them, and in like manner the fish. ¹⁴This was now the third time Jesus was revealed to his disciples after being raised from the dead.

Jesus and Peter. ¹⁵When they had finished breakfast, Jesus said to Simon Peter, "Simon, son of John, do you love me more than these?" He said to him, "Yes, Lord, you know that I love you." He said to him, "Feed my lambs." ¹⁶He then said to him a second time, "Simon, son of John, do you love me?" He said to him, "Yes, Lord, you know that I love you." He said to him, "Tend my sheep." ¹⁷He said to him the third time, "Simon, son of John, do you love me?" Peter was dis-

bolic; and St. Jerome may have the key when he tells us that for the Greek zoologists there were just 153 kinds of fish. At the beginning of the Synoptic ministry, Jesus had promised to make the apostles "fishers of men"; now with his help they catch every type of fish in their net. In this prophetic action, John sees the disciples being commissioned to gather and draw in people, a commission that for Matthew is the essence of the Galilean appearances. Luke, having no Galilean appearances, has no room in the post-resurrection account for this miraculous catch of fish. And so, where does he narrate it (or, at least, a scene that is virtually identical)?—in the story of the call of the apostles and the promise to make them fishers for human beings (thus connecting the two events). *Mk 1:17; Ez 47:9-10 Mt 13:47-48; 28:16-20 Lk 5:1-11*

13 The account of Jesus' taking the bread and fish and giving them to the disciples has the same vocabulary as the scene in c. 6 (the only other scene in John on the shore of the lake). We saw eucharistic significance there, and we may *suspect* its presence here, after the commission to the disciples. *#4? Jn 6:11*

Peter's profession of love—21:15-19

The next scene concerns the threefold test of Peter. As many Fathers have seen, we have here a reparation for the threefold denial at Annas' house. When his denial was prophesied at the Last Supper, Peter was sure he knew better than Jesus what he would do, and Peter boasted that he would follow Jesus. *Jn 13:37-38*

15-17 Only his threefold admission that Jesus knows his heart can gain him the chance actually to follow (v. 19). In commenting on c. 10, we referred to the authoritative role of the shepherd-ruler in the Old Testament. In this tradition, Jesus presented himself as the Good Shepherd who lays down his life for his sheep. At the Last Supper Peter boasted he was willing to lay down his life. Jesus, about to leave his sheep (sheep that he *Jn 10:11 Jn 13:37*

tressed that he had said to him a third time, "Do you love me?" and he said to him, "Lord, you know everything; you know that I love you." [Jesus] said to him, "Feed my sheep. [18]Amen, amen, I say to you, when you were younger, you used to dress yourself and go where you wanted; but when you grow old, you will stretch out your hands, and someone else will dress you and lead you where you do not want to go." [19]He said this signifying by what kind of death he would glorify God. And when he had said this, he said to him, "Follow me."

The Beloved Disciple. [20]Peter turned and saw the disciple following whom Jesus loved, the one who had also reclined upon his chest during the supper and had said, "Master, who is the one who will betray you?" [21]When Peter saw him, he said to Jesus, "Lord, what about him?" [22]Jesus said to him, "What if I want him to remain until I come? What concern is it of yours? You follow me." [23]So the word spread among the brothers that that disciple would not die. But Jesus had not told him that he would not die, just "What if I want him to remain until I come? [What concern is it of yours?]"

Conclusion. [24]It is this disciple who testifies to these things and has written them, and we know that his testimony is true.

willed to form into one flock under one shepherd), first insists on the Johannine criterion of love, and then makes Peter a shepherd—but the sheep remain Jesus'. As shepherd Peter will have his chance to lay down his life. As a youth he was his own impetuous master; but in his old age, his hands will be stretched on the cross, whither he will follow his master. The editor points out the hidden meaning of this prophecy, probably impressed by its awesome accuracy, since, for the editor, Peter's crucifixion on Vatican hill was already history.

Jn 10:16

18

19

John—21:20-23

Ever close to Peter, the beloved disciple appears in the final scene. His fate, too, is the subject of an enigmatic saying. While the Lord's answer is not much more than a "None of your business" to the ever-rash Peter, it was (by the editor's time) misunderstood by some as a prediction of the disciple's living until the second coming of Jesus. We must remember the ardent and imminent expectation of the parousia in the early church. Many may have misunderstood the words, "This generation will not pass away till all these things be accomplished," and believed that the apostles would not all die before Jesus returned. But Johannine Christians applied this hope to the beloved disciple; with his death the faith of some was shaken. And so this incident is narrated to clarify the difficulty.

2 Th 2
Mt 24:34

Attesting signature—21:24-25

The added chapter closes with an assurance that the witness who stands behind the narrative of the Gospel is the beloved

²⁵There are also many other things that Jesus did, but if these were to be described individually, I do not think the whole world would contain the books that would be written.

disciple—he is responsible for its writing (perhaps by supplying the witness or testimony embodied in it) and his witness is true. And, finally, the actual scribe adds a note explaining that not everything has been written. The whole Jesus cannot be captured in the pages of a book, even a book such as the Fourth Gospel.

The Epistles of John

Introduction

Authorship of First, Second, Third John

Second and Third John are alike in letter format, especially in the Opening and Closing; plausibly they are the work of the same "presbyter" and may have been written about the same time. Second John has similarities of content to First John (which has no letter format), especially in 2 John 5-7 which emphasizes the commandment to love one another (1 Jn 2:7-11) and condemns the deceivers (antichrist) who have gone forth into the world (1 Jn 2:18-19). Thus, though the writer of First John does not identify himself, most scholars think that the presbyter composed all three works.

Relation of the Epistles to the Gospel

In writing style and vocabulary there are very many similarities between the Epistles and the Fourth Gospel, but also a few surprising differences:

(a) The prologue of First John emphasizes not the incarnation of the personified Word, but testimony to the word (message) of life which was seen, heard, and felt—the human career of Jesus.

(b) Features which the Gospel attributes to Jesus are assigned in First John to God, e.g., in 1:5 God is light (see Jn 8:12); in 4:21 and 2 John 4 God gives the commandment to love one another (see Jn 13:34). One may speak of a lower christology in the Epistles.

(c) There is less epistolary emphasis on the Spirit as a person, and the Gospel term "Paraclete" is never used of the Spirit. (Christ is the paraclete or advocate in 1 Jn 2:1.) There is a warning that every spirit is not the Spirit of Truth or the Spirit of God, and so spirits must be tested (4:1, 6).

(d) Final eschatology is stronger in First John than in John where realized eschatology dominates. There is more emphasis on the parousia as the moment of accountability for Christian life (1 Jn 2:28–3:3).

(e) The Dead Sea Scroll parallels, especially as to vocabulary, are even closer in First John than in John.

Some of these differences give the Epistles the air of being more primitive than the Gospel, but they may reflect the author's claim to be presenting the gospel as it was "from the beginning" (1 Jn 1:1; 3:11). They suggest that the same author may not have written the Gospel and the Epistles. Overall, then, we may distinguish *at least four figures in the Johannine School* responsible for the Gospel and Epistles: the beloved disciple (who was the source of the tradition), the evangelist, the presbyter of the Epistles, and the redactor of the Gospel. Most scholars think the Epistles were written after the Gospel. More precisely, I would place them in the decade after the body of the Gospel was written by the evangelist (ca. 90) but before the redaction of the Gospel (just after 100?).

Occasion of the Epistles

What particularly differentiates First and Second John from the Gospel is the change of focus. "The Jews" who are the chief adversaries in the Gospel are absent, and all attention is on deceivers who have seceded from the community (1 Jn 2:19; 2 Jn 7) and by so doing have shown a lack of love for their former brethren. Such "antichrists" would seduce the writer's adherents on several issues:

Faith. The secessionists deny that *Jesus* is the Christ, the Son of God (2:22-23). Since they were Johannine Christians who believed in Jesus, presumably the denial attributed to them means that they negated the importance of Jesus by not confessing him as the Christ come in the flesh (4:3). Probably they thought that salvation came solely from the entrance of the Son of God into the world, so that the historical career of Jesus had no salvific importance. In particular, they may have neglected the atoning bloody death of Jesus which the author emphasizes (1:7; 2:2; 4:10; 5:6).

Morals. They (presumably the same group) boast of being in communion with God and knowing God while walking in darkness and not keeping the commandments (1:6; 2:4); indeed, they claim not to have sinned (1:8, 10; 3:4-6). This moral stance may be related to their christology if, having denied the importance of what Jesus did in the flesh after the incarnation of the Son, they denied the importance of what they themselves did in the flesh after becoming children of God through belief. The author insists that the true child of God does not sin (3:9-10; 5:18) and keeps the commandments, especially the commandment to love one's fellow Christian (3:11, 23; 2 Jn 5). The children of God must walk in purity and love just as did Jesus, God's Son (2:6; 3:3, 7; 4:10-11).

Spirit. Seemingly the secessionist leaders claim to be teachers and even prophets, led by the Spirit. The author disclaims the need for teachers (2:27) and warns against false prophets. He mentions the latter as he warns, "Do not believe every spirit, but test the spirits to see whether they are of God" (4:1). There is a Spirit of Deceit that leads the antichrists, and a Spirit of Truth that leads the author and his adherents (4:5-6).

There have been attempts to identify the secessionist adversaries of the Epistles with known "heretics," e.g., the *docetists* attacked by Ignatius of Antioch (ca. 110) who denied that Christ was truly human; or *Cerinthus* (described by Irenaeus as an opponent of John) who held that the Christ, a spiritual being, descended upon Jesus, a normal man, after baptism and withdrew from him before crucifixion; or second-century *gnostics* who regarded the world and flesh as a deception.

Such known heresies, however, may be later descendants of the error encountered in the Epistles. *That error is plausibly an exaggeration by Johannine Christians of certain features in the Fourth Gospel.* For instance, the Gospel portrays the incarnation of the pre-existent Son of God who saves people by his very coming into the world as the light— anyone who comes to the light is free from being judged and from the guilt of sin (Jn 3:16-21; 9:39-41). Since people seemed to be saved by faith during the ministry of Jesus, it is not emphasized in John that the death of Jesus is salvific. The Gospel gives little ethical teaching except the commandment to love one another. According to John 14:16, 17, 26; 16:13, the Paraclete (advocate) or Spirit of Truth comes to dwell in every believer, guiding that person to all truth.

Despite the possibility of developing such Gospel themes to produce the views held by the secessionists, the author of First and Second John claims that his views and not those of the secessionists represent the true "gospel" held from the beginning. (The word translated "message" in 1:5 and 3:11 is *angelia*, possibly the Johannine equivalent for "gospel" or *euangelion*.) He belongs to the Johannine School who bears witness to the tradition that comes down from the beloved disciple—a "we" who personally or by association have heard, seen, looked upon, and felt Jesus, the embodiment of the life of God (1 Jn 1:1); a "we" who know the importance of how Jesus lived (walked) in the flesh and died for sins. The differences of thought from the Gospel described above make sense as a reaction to the misinterpretation of the Gospel by the secessionists.

First John, then, would not be a letter or epistle, but an exhortation interpreting the main themes of the Fourth Gospel in light of secessionist propaganda which had a certain plausibility and continued to attract followers. Presumably it was circulated in the main center of Johannine Christianity where the Gospel was written and the author lived.

Second John is a true letter sent by the author to a Johannine community at a distance from the center. The secession had not yet reached there, but secessionist missionaries were on the way (2 Jn 9-10). Writing as a disciple of the beloved disciple (for which role "presbyter" was a technical title), the author instructs that community (the Elect Lady and her children) not to let such false teachers into "the house" (church where the community met). The arrival of emissaries, some from the presbyter, some from the secessionists, must have been confusing to such distant Johannine communities. How were they to know who carried the truth until they allowed the emissaries to speak? And by then the damage was done!

In one community a certain Diotrephes emerged as a local leader and decided to keep out such missionaries, including those from the presbyter. His refusal of hospitality causes the presbyter to write **Third John** to Gaius, seemingly a wealthy person in a neighboring community. Gaius has been providing hospitality on a temporary basis, but the presbyter wants him to take over responsibility for helping the missionaries and thus (seemingly) open a rival house church to that of Diotrephes. The missionaries from the presbyter (such as Demetrius who is about to come) spread the true interpretation of the Johannine Gospel; and by helping them, Gaius becomes a fellow-worker for the truth. Although attacked for "loving to have first place," Diotrephes may have been shrewder than the presbyter in recognizing that an authoritative local orthodox teacher was a surer protection against Spirit-led false prophets than were missionaries exhorting people to test the spirits. Diotrephes may have been an early Johannine representative of the bishop-teacher who was emerging or already established in the non-Johannine Christian communities of what Ignatius of Antioch calls "the Church Catholic."

Outline of First John

Scholars disagree on this issue, for the author is repetitious and seemingly without a clear plan. A tripartite division is popular (Three Parts, preceded by a Prologue and followed by an Epilogue). Because I believe that First John is an interpretation of the Fourth Gospel, I favor a bipartite division that corresponds to the Gospel division given above on pp. 15–16. A Prologue (1:1-4) comments on the hymn that is the Gospel Prologue (Jn 1:1-18), and a Conclusion (5:13-21) draws on the theme of the preredactional Gospel Conclusion (Jn 20:30-31). The two main Parts of the Epistle are marked off by the statement "This is the gospel" (*angelia*, "message") in 1:5 and 3:11. Part One (1:5–3:10) defines the gospel as "God is light" and stresses the obligation of walking in light. Part Two (3:11–5:12) defines the gospel as "We should love one another" and holds up Jesus as the example of love for one's brother and sister.

The First Epistle of John

Text and Commentary

I. PROLOGUE

The Word of Life

1 ¹What was from the beginning,
what we have heard,
what we have seen with our eyes,
what we looked upon
and touched with our hands
concerns the Word of life—
²for the life was made visible;
we have seen it and testify to it

and proclaim to you the eternal life
that was with the Father and was made
visible to us—
³what we have seen and heard
we proclaim now to you,
so that you too may have fellowship
with us;
for our fellowship is with the Father
and with his Son, Jesus Christ.
⁴We are writing this so that our joy may
be complete.

PROLOGUE

1 Jn 1:1-4

The prologue to First John resembles a primitive sketch of the prologue to the Fourth Gospel. We say "primitive," for we certainly do not find here the clarity found in the Gospel. Dominant is the importance of the "we," namely, the tradition bearers and interpreters of the Johannine School who preserve and develop the (eye)witness of the beloved disciple. (The "beginning" refers to the start of Jesus' ministry where such witness played a role.) The object of the eyewitnessing is "the word of life," but with more emphasis on "life" than on "word." In the prologue of John it is the *Word* who was made flesh and whose glory we saw; here it is the *life* that was made known. First John seems to give an intermediary stage in the use of "word" less personalized than in John: "the word of life" means more than simply the news or message about the divine life; yet it is less than the incarnate Word that possesses and gives life in the Fourth Gospel. It seems to mean the proclamation of divine life (v. 2) made visible in and through Jesus. The "word" is the *angelia* or "message" of 1 Jn 1:5; 3:11 which enables the readers to participate in this life, and thus have fellowship with the living God. (*Koinonia* or "fellowship"—associating and sharing goods and life—is a Pauline word that does not occur in John.) This fellowship is

Marginal references:

1 — Jn 19:35; 21:24; Jn 20:29; Jn 1:14

2-3 — Mt 13:19; 2 Tim 2:15; Jn 1:4; Jn 14:6; 1 Jn 5:11-12; Jn 20:31; 1 Cor 1:9; Phil 3:10

II. GOD AS LIGHT

God is Light. [5]Now this is the message that we have heard from him and proclaim to you: God is light, and in him there is no darkness at all. [6]If we say, "We have fellowship with him," while we continue to walk in darkness, we lie and do not act in truth. [7]But if we walk in the light as he is in the light, then we have fellowship with one another, and the blood of his Son Jesus cleanses us from all sin. [8]If we say, "We are without sin," we deceive ourselves, and the truth is not in us. [9]If we acknowledge our sins, he is faithful and just and will forgive our sins and cleanse us from every wrongdoing. [10]If we say, "We have not sinned," we make him a liar, and his word is not in us.

2 Christ and His Commandments. [1]My children, I am writing this to you

the root of Christian joy and an essential constituent of the Johannine community ("with us"). Jn 15:11

PART ONE—WALK IN THE LIGHT OF GOD

1 Jn 1:5–3:10

Walking in light—1:5-7

The author begins with the particular aspect of the Christian life he wishes to emphasize. In his view of a world divided into light and darkness, God is the light of the just who walk in paths brightened by his rays. As usual, darkness is evil. This world picture, as well as the expressions "walk in light" and "do the truth," is reminiscent of Dead Sea Scrolls phraseology. Basically the walking in light which guarantees Christian fellowship consists in keeping the commandments; it is an echo of Part I of the Last Discourse where we heard that union with God means keeping the commandments. (But we do not have the developed Triadic outlook of the Last Discourse; the three specific divine figures are not mentioned, only "fellowship with *him*.")

See p. 37
Ps 27:1

Cf. p. 14

Cf. p. 76

6-7

Opposition to sin—1:8-2:2

The writer then turns to the thought of sin, and to the false propagandists who refuse to acknowledge their wrongdoing as sin. True Christians before God admit their sins, *acknowledging* or publicly confessing them (the Council of Trent cited this text in relation to confession). Such humble confession gains forgiveness through the blood of Jesus (v. 7). To claim sinlessness is to make a liar out of God who sent his Son to redeem us from sin, and thus to equate him with Satan, the liar *par excellence.* Surely First John does not wish to encourage

DBS 1679
Heb 9:13-
14, 22;
Ap 5:9

Jn 8:44

9

2:1

so that you may not commit sin. But if anyone does sin, we have an Advocate with the Father, Jesus Christ the righteous one. ²He is expiation for our sins, and not for our sins only but for those of the whole world. ³The way we may be sure that we know him is to keep his commandments. ⁴Whoever says, "I know him," but does not keep his commandments is a liar, and the truth is not in him. ⁵But whoever keeps his word, the love of God is truly perfected in him. This is the way we may know that we are in union with him: ⁶whoever claims to abide in him ought to live [just] as he lived.

The New Commandment. ⁷Beloved, I am writing no new commandment to you but an old commandment that you had from the beginning. The old commandment is the word that you have heard. ⁸And yet I do write a new commandment to you, which holds true in him and among you, for the darkness is passing away, and the true light is already shining. ⁹Whoever says he is in the light, yet hates his brother, is still in the darkness.

2   sin; but the greatest weapon against sin is its recognition and a dependence on the redemption wrought by Jesus. The propitiatory quality of Jesus' death is emphasized in First John more than in John. The Lamb of God takes away the world's sins, not only by destroying evil, but by expiating for them through his death. Notice that in this Epistle Jesus is the paraclete ("advocate"), a title which the Gospel applies to the Spirit.

Cf. Jn 1:29
1 Jn 3:5;
4:10
Cf. Jn
14:16

Keeping the commandments—2:3-11

First John now specifically emphasizes the theme of keeping the commandments in order to know God (the Semitic idea of knowledge implies intimacy), virtually repeating Part I of the
4   Last Discourse. This theme is directed against the false propa-
5   gandists (notice the "whoever says" in verses 4, 6, 9). Love of God—perhaps in the twofold sense of the love of God for us, and our love for God—is the perfection effected by keeping the commandments, and indeed the index of our union with
6   God. Verse 6 makes no effort to distinguish between God (the Father—"abide in *him*") and Jesus ("as *he* walked [lived]"); perhaps the reason behind this ambiguity is the conviction that Jesus and the Father are one.
7   The thoughts of love and of commandments introduce the
8   great commandment of the Last Supper. This was a commandment that John's children had heard from their first conversion, but which was yet to be put into effect in a world liberated by Jesus from the power of darkness. The self-sacrificing love of Christians for one another, based on Jesus' love for them, was a novelty which caused the Gentiles to exclaim: "See how
9-11   these Christians love one another." The failure to keep this great commandment of love removes one from the sphere of the light

Jn 14:15,
21-24

#3?

Jn 10:30;
14:9-10

Jn 13:34
Jn 16:33

Jn 8:12;

111

¹⁰Whoever loves his brother remains in the light, and there is nothing in him to cause a fall. ¹¹Whoever hates his brother is in darkness; he walks in darkness and does not know where he is going because the darkness has blinded his eyes.

Members of the Community. ¹²I am writing to you, children, because your sins have been forgiven for his name's sake.

¹³I am writing to you, fathers, because you know him who is from the beginning.

I am writing to you, young men, because you have conquered the evil one.

¹⁴I write to you, children, because you know the Father.

I write to you, fathers, because you know him who is from the beginning.

I write to you, young men, because you are strong and the word of God remains in you, and you have conquered the evil one.

¹⁵Do not love the world or the things of the world. If anyone loves the world, the love of the Father is not in him. ¹⁶For all that is in the world, sensual lust, enticement for the eyes, and a pretentious life, is not from the Father but is from the

of Jesus. (The phrase in v. 8 concerning "the true light" reminds us of John's prologue.)

11:10
Jn 1:9

Opposition to the world—2:12-17

Verses 12-14 are very difficult; the word translated "because" may also mean "that,"and thus give a different connotation. Three titles are dealt with (children, fathers, young men) in two sequences (verses 12-13, and verse 14). The *children* may be taken as a general term of address, including the fathers and young men. The two main assurances to the children in verses 12, 14 concern the principal difficulties with the false propagandists, namely, the forgiveness of sins, and true knowledge of the Father. The *fathers* (who have been Christian longer) are appropriately connected with knowledge of the One who is from the beginning; the *young people* (recent Christians) are appropriately connected with temptation and strength (in overcoming Satan). Probably, in poetic style, verse 14 is only repeating verses 12-13. In verses 12-13 the Christians' sins are forgiven through Jesus, the revelation of the eternal life of the Father, who has conquered Satan. In verse 14 the Christians know the Father through the revelation of eternal life of the Father in Jesus, who is the abiding word of God and helps Christians to overcome Satan.

Tit 2:1-8

Jn 1:1;
1 Jn 1:1
Lk
11:21-22

15 The thought of the evil one leads to the thought of his domain, the world. In the Last Discourse (Part III), Jesus said that he was not of this world, nor should his followers be of this
16 world. Therefore, any love for the world disbars one from following Jesus. First John's three characteristic notes of the world hav become well-known as concupiscence, envy, and pride, the constituents of the first of that larger evil triad: the world,

Lk 4:6;
Jn 12:31
1 Jn 5:19
Jn
17:14-16

world. ¹⁷Yet the world and its enticement are passing away. But whoever does the will of God remains forever.

Antichrists. ¹⁸Children, it is the last hour; and just as you heard that the antichrist was coming, so now many antichrists have appeared. Thus we know this is the last hour. ¹⁹They went out from us, but they were not really of our number; if they had been, they would have remained with us. Their desertion shows that none of them was of our number. ²⁰But you have the anointing that comes from the holy one, and you all have knowledge. ²¹I write to you not because you do not know the truth but because you do, and because every lie is alien to the truth. ²²Who is the liar? Whoever denies that Jesus is the Christ. Whoever denies the Father and the Son, this is the antichrist. ²³No one who denies the Son has the Father, but whoever confesses the Son has the Father as well.

Life from God's Anointing. ²⁴Let what you heard from the beginning remain in you. If what you heard from the begin-

17   the flesh, and the devil. However, our author does not give us an exhaustive catalogue of sinful tendencies found in the world, but simply characterizes the sensual, materialistic pagan society that Christianity had to overcome. Of its nature, such a world is transitory.

Antichrists—2:18-27

The thought of the transitory nature of the world leads to the thought of its end. For John's partially realized eschatology, #5 the present is the last hour, since the apocalyptic struggle between Satan and Christ, in the persons of the false propagandists and the true Christians, is already in process. (First John's interpretation of the traditional antichrist ["as you have heard"] Mt 24:24; to be the false teachers of his time *may* represent a reinterpre- 1 Tim 4:1ff tation of the expectation of one monstrous personification of 2 Th 2:3ff

19   evil.) Those who are against (anti-) Christ are former nominal Johannine Christians who have openly left the fold. They
22-23   now have joined the ranks of the great liar, Satan, by denying that Jesus is the Christ (come in the flesh; see 4:3). To them may be applied the eternally true criterion of Christianity (to which all "Christians" should submit): if one denies the Son, one denies the Father, because the Son is our chief means of knowing the Father.

20-21   Yet John does not really need to tell his children this for they have all been anointed by God (Father or Son or both?) with the Holy Spirit sent in the name of Jesus to teach all things and to interpret the truth about the Son. First John seeks to 1 Th 4:8-9 combine the idea of the Spirit teaching the individual with the Jn 14:26;
24   authoritative guide of tradition: "what you have heard from 16:13-15 the beginning." The anointing with the Spirit enables individuals to adhere to the truth of the teaching received and thus

ning remains in you, then you will remain in the Son and in the Father. ²⁵And this is the promise that he made us: eternal life. ²⁶I write you these things about those who would deceive you. ²⁷As for you, the anointing that you received from him remains in you, so that you do not need anyone to teach you. But his anointing teaches you about everything and is true and not false; just as it taught you, remain in him.

Children of God. ²⁸And now, children, remain in him, so that when he appears we may have confidence and not be put to shame by him at his coming. ²⁹If you consider that he is righteous, you also know that everyone who acts in righteousness is begotten by him.

3 ¹See what love the Father has bestowed on us that we may be called the children of God. Yet so we are. The reason the world does not know us is that

25   maintains them in eternal life, the intimate knowledge of the   Jn 17:3
26-27   Father and the Son. In this sense, the anointing with the Spirit obviates the need for human teachers, including the secessionist propagandists (2 Jn 9–10). Through Spirit-anointing, the Christian is truly taught by God. We should notice in this passage that while the Spirit is clearly implied, the word "Spirit" is not mentioned—only the "anointing" which abides in the Christian. Is the author avoiding John's language of the Paraclete-Spirit because secessionists appeal to it? Perhaps too anointing (verses 20, 27) is a reflection on the baptized state of First John's children.

     Jn 6:45;
     2 Cor 1:22

     Acts 10:38;
     Lk 4:18
     Acts 1:5

Children of God—2:28–3:3

Verse 28 both ends the section on the last hour begun in 2:18 and turns to the idea of union with God and Jesus. The parousia or return of Jesus at the end of time is not too frequent a thought in John, as distinct from First John. The true connection between realized and final eschatology is that, while Jesus is present to each Christian who does justice, the fulness of
29   union is possible only with his final return. Present union with him enables one to face with confidence his return in judgment (either in death or at the end of the world). The idea of "being begotten by him" (probably the Father; notice the confusing shifting between the Father and Jesus) is the underlying presupposition of acting righteously; the Father's love is always the
3:1   source of sanctification. As we read, "See what love the Father has *given* us," we should think of Jesus, the fount of our sonship, the incarnate love of God *given* for us. The world is incapable of knowing God (another Last Discourse theme), and therefore incapable of knowing his children, who resemble
2   him. At the return of Jesus, the only natural Son, when the children see God as he is, the resemblance will be even closer.

     Col 3:4;
     1 Cor 1:7
     #5
     Jn 5:26-
     30; 14:1-3

     Cf. Jn
     1:12-13

     Jn 3:16
     Cf. Jn
     14:22-24
     Jn 17:25
     1 Cor
     13:12;

it did not know him. ²Beloved, we are God's children now; what we shall be has not yet been revealed. We do know that when it is revealed we shall be like him, for we shall see him as he is. ³Everyone who has this hope based on him makes himself pure, as he is pure.

Avoiding Sin. ⁴Everyone who commits sin commits lawlessness, for sin is lawlessness. ⁵You know that he was revealed to take away sins, and in him there is no sin. ⁶No one who remains in him sins; no one who sins has seen him or known him. ⁷Children, let no one deceive you. The person who acts in righteousness is righteous, just as he is righteous. ⁸Whoever sins belongs to the devil, because the devil has sinned from the beginning. Indeed, the Son of God was revealed to destroy the works of the devil. ⁹No one who is begotten by God commits sin, because God's seed remains in him; he cannot sin because he is begotten by God. ¹⁰In this way, the children of God and the children of the devil are made plain; no one who fails to act in righteousness belongs to God, nor anyone who does not love his brother.

3	Sanctity is our best preparation for being like God, and for seeing him.	2 Cor 3:18 Jn 6:46 Mt 5:8

Avoiding sin—3:4-10

Sin is the great obstacle to being a child of God. (By stressing that sin is *iniquity* ["lawlessness"]), First John may mean that sin is the mark of the children of Satan; recall the "man of iniquity" and the "mystery of iniquity.") Despite the claims of the false propagandists, the sinner has no intimacy with Jesus who takes sin away. If the child of God is marked by freedom from sin, the child of the devil is marked by sin. God is just; the devil, a sinner; the children are like the father. First John's world, divided into two hostile groups, is again reminiscent of Qumran. The idea that a child of God cannot sin does not contradict 1:8. In principle, the Johannine Christians hold sin as something evil, while the secessionists think it does not affect union with God. The author knows that at times the Christian will sin, but this is in spite of, and not because of, being a child of God. Notice how realistically First John treats our rebirth from God: we have God's *seed* in us (v. 9), i.e., the Holy Spirit, the breath of life he has given us.

Margin references: 5-6 2 Th 2:3-7; 7 Jn 1:29; 8:46; 9 Cf. p. 14; 10 1 Pt 1:23; 1 Jn 3:24 Cf. Jn 20:21-22

PART TWO—WALK AS CHILDREN OF THE GOD OF LOVE

1 Jn 3:11–5:12

Keep the commandments—3:11-24

Once again we hear the *angelia* ("message, gospel"), now in terms of love (instead of light); hatred is the mark of the evil

Margin reference: 1 Jn 1:5

III: LOVE FOR ONE ANOTHER

¹¹For this is the message you have heard from the beginning: we should love one another, ¹²unlike Cain who belonged to the evil one and slaughtered his brother. Why did he slaughter him? Because his own works were evil, and those of his brother righteous. ¹³Do not be amazed, [then,] brothers, if the world hates you. ¹⁴We know that we have passed from death to life because we love our brothers. Whoever does not love remains in death. ¹⁵Everyone who hates his brother is a murderer, and you know that no murderer has eternal life remaining in him. ¹⁶The way we came to know love was that he laid down his life for us; so we ought to lay down our lives for our brothers. ¹⁷If someone who has worldly means sees a brother in need and refuses him compassion, how can the love of God remain in him? ¹⁸Children, let us love not in word or speech but in deed and truth.

Confidence before God. ¹⁹[Now] this is how we shall know that we belong to the truth and reassure our hearts before him ²⁰in whatever our hearts condemn, for God is greater than our hearts and knows everything. ²¹Beloved, if [our] hearts do not condemn us, we have confidence in God ²²and receive from him whatever we ask, because we keep his commandments and do what pleases him. ²³And his commandment is this: we should believe in the name of his Son, Jesus Christ, and love one another just as he commanded us. ²⁴Those who keep his commandments

one's children (like Cain) and of his domain, the world. Love

14-15 is the great sign of having passed out of the kingdom of Satan, the kingdom of death. For hatred is a form of murder and marked with death. When Satan entered into Judas, he be-

16 trayed Jesus to death. Jesus conquered death by laying down his life voluntarily, and taking it up again. That was the supreme example of love; and if we wish to follow, we too must love, not only theoretically, but practically. The specification

17-18 of love as helping a "brother in need," if directed against the secessionists of 2:19, suggests they were the wealthier members of the community, helping to explain why they are equated with the world.

19 The "this" of v. 19 can refer to what has just been said (by a practice of love) or to what follows (by the greatness of God). If we choose the former, the practice of love assures Christians

20 that they are on God's side ("of the truth"). If they are aware of past sin, their heart can be easy; for God knows their weakness, and God's powerful mercy can forgive sin. If their life

21 has been just, they can have even more confidence in God.

22 Keeping the commandments is the supreme source of our confident calling on God (again we meet themes of the Last Dis-

23 course). And the summation of the commandments is to believe in Jesus and to love one another—the very points of faith and practice in which the false propagandists are deficient. (Notice the emphasis on *the name* of Jesus, a favorite theme of

24 John's Gospel.) As at the Last Supper, we hear that keeping

Jn 8:44;
Wis 2:24

Jn 13:2, 27
Jn 10:17-
18; Rom
5:21

Jn 15:13

Mk 10:21;
Acts
2:44-45

Acts 24:16

Jn 14:13-
15; 16:23

Jn 1:12;
2:23

remain in him, and he in them, and the way we know that he remains in us is from the Spirit that he gave us.

4 **Testing the Spirits.** ¹Beloved, do not trust every spirit but test the spirits to see whether they belong to God, because many false prophets have gone out into the world. ²This is how you can know the Spirit of God: every spirit that acknowledges Jesus Christ come in the flesh belongs to God, ³and every spirit that does not acknowledge Jesus does not belong to God. This is the spirit of the antichrist that, as you heard, is to come, but in fact is already in the world. ⁴You belong to God, children, and you have conquered them, for the one who is in you is greater than the one who is in the world. ⁵They belong to the world; accordingly, their teaching belongs to the world, and the world listens to them. ⁶We belong to God, and anyone who knows God listens to us, while anyone who does not belong to God refuses to hear us. This is how we know the spirit of truth and the spirit of deceit.

God's Love and Christian Life. ⁷Beloved, let us love one another, because

the commandments will lead to the divine presence (again Father and Son are not distinguished). It is the Spirit who gives testimony of this divine presence, the Spirit who, it was promised, would be sent to give testimony. See p. 76 Rom 8:14-16; Gal 4:6; Jn 15:26

Test the spirits—4:1-6

Yet the author is too wise a pastor to allow his children to fall back on any vague witness of the "Spirit." Therefore he urges a test, basically a test of "By their fruits you shall know them." One's spirit or tendency will betray itself in one's actions. The

2 mark of the spirit (or Spirit?—the word wanders from an impersonal to a personal sense) of God is belief that Jesus is

3 the Messiah or Christ incarnate. The false propagandists are really destroying Jesus in neglecting his human career and so are of an anti-Christ spirit, a spirit already in the world. These

4 are dangerous adversaries; but the Christian can conquer

5-6 them because Jesus has conquered Satan. And so once again Jn 16:33 John comes to his picture of a divided humankind: some standing with God and marked by a spirit of truth, separated from a world which is against God and marked by a spirit of deceit. There are strong parallels to the Qumran world-picture where 1QS 3, 18-19 people are dominated by a spirit of truth and a spirit of deceit. (The expression "to test the spirits" occurs in the Dead Sea 1QS 5, 20-21 Scrolls in reference to new members of the community.) At the end of this section First John comes to the ultimate test of truth and deceit: the ability "to listen to us," i.e., conformity with the witness of the Johannine School. Of course, one may guess that the secessionists are directing the same polemic against the author and his followers; for them *he* has the spirit of deceit.

love is of God; everyone who loves is be-gotten by God and knows God. ⁸Who-ever is without love does not know God, for God is love. ⁹In this way the love of God was revealed to us: God sent his only Son into the world so that we might have life through him. ¹⁰In this is love: not that we have loved God, but that he loved us and sent his Son as expi-ation for our sins. ¹¹Beloved, if God so loved us, we also must love one another. ¹²No one has ever seen God. Yet, if we love one another, God remains in us, and his love is brought to perfection in us.

¹³This is how we know that we remain in him and he in us, that he has given us of his Spirit. ¹⁴Moreover, we have seen and testify that the Father sent his Son as savior of the world. ¹⁵Whoever ac-knowledges that Jesus is the Son of God, God remains in him and he in God. ¹⁶We have come to know and to believe in the love God has for us.

God is love, and whoever remains in love remains in God and God in him. ¹⁷In this is love brought to perfection among us, that we have confidence on the day of judgment because as he is, so are we

Love—4:7–5:4

Abruptly First John returns to the theme of love for one an-other. "God is love," he tells us, i.e., love characterizes his deal- Cf. Jn 4:24
ings with us. (The God of the Old Testament and of the New Testament is a God who has made himself known by *acting* in history. If we ask what this God is, the answer comes back
9 in terms of what he does.) With love he has sent his Son, Jn 3:16
10 not a love corresponding to love on our part, but an entirely Ps 145:8-9
gratuitous love—a love for sinners. This concept of God's love, Rom 5:8
embodied in Jesus' self-giving, is the unique possession of
11 Christianity, the greatest proof of its truth. The only require- Jn 17:26
ment attached to this gift of love is that of sharing it with others.
12 The love for others brings us as close as we can come on earth Jn 1:18;
to union with the God we cannot see. This statement may be 6:46
an attack on the secessionists, who claimed special knowledge
and visions of God. (Notice how First John's theology of love
resembles St. Thomas' teaching that in this life we come closer
to God through love than through knowledge.)
13 The author repeats that the Spirit is our pledge of union 1 Jn 3:24
with God. (Theology tells us that the Spirit is the love existing
between the Father and the Son, and thus the ideal witness of
14 our union with God through love.) Returning to the supreme
example of love, the author testifies to the reality of the send-
15-16 ing of the Son as savior. Belief in this act of love, and abiding in love are the two conditions of God's abiding in us.
17 The "in this" of v. 17 is again vague; it may refer to what has
been said (abiding in God), or to what follows (confidence).
In any case the perfection of love is connected to our confidence on the day of judgment, confidence based on our resemblance on earth to our judge (presumably Jesus). The children

in this world. ¹⁸There is no fear in love, but perfect love drives out fear because fear has to do with punishment, and so one who fears is not yet perfect in love. ¹⁹We love because he first loved us. ²⁰If anyone says, "I love God," but hates his brother, he is a liar; for whoever does not love a brother whom he has seen cannot love God whom he has not seen. ²¹This is the commandment we have from him: whoever loves God must also love his brother.

5 Faith is Victory over the World. ¹Everyone who believes that Jesus is

the Christ is begotten by God, and everyone who loves the father loves [also] the one begotten by him. ²In this way we know that we love the children of God when we love God and obey his commandments. ³For the love of God is this, that we keep his commandments. And his commandments are not burdensome, ⁴for whoever is begotten by God conquers the world. And the victory that conquers the world is our faith. ⁵Who [indeed] is the victor over the world but the one who believes that Jesus is the Son of God?

⁶This is the one who came through

18 of God who pattern themselves on their Father need not have an overpowering or servile fear of judgment. (First John does not deal with reverential fear, which is good, but with the servile fear which marks God's enemies.) Those who resemble God most, i.e., those who are perfected in love, need not cower at his coming. Those who are still imperfect fear God's punish-   `Mt 10:28`

19-20 ment. Therefore we should perfect ourselves in love for one another, the test of our love for God. This test cannot be met by the secessionists who hate their former brothers in the

21 Johannine Community. Verse 21 is the foundation of the Christian emphasis on the role of charity in the spiritual life; but notice always the Johannine restriction of love to one's community members.   `Jn 13:34; Mk 12:29-31`

5:1-2 The connection between the two essentials, faith and love, is now introduced. Correct belief in Jesus makes one a child of God. If we love God, we should love his children who are   `Jn 1:12`

3 like him. Love, both of the Father and of the children, is marked by keeping the commandments. Here the author is warning that gestures of charity are insufficient unless accompanied by sanctity of life. Even the philanthropist cannot escape the obligation to live a holy life. These commandments are not a burden like those of the Pharisees; for the world whose lusts   `Jn 14:15; 15:10`   `Mt 11:28-30; 23:4`

4 and attractions could be an obstacle to keeping the commandments has been conquered. Jesus has overcome the world, and our faith in him enables us to conquer the world.   `1 Jn 2:15-17; 4:4`   `Ap 2:7, 11`

Witnesses to the faith—5:6-12

6 Then the author, thinking of the beloved disciple at the cross, recalls the scene of Jesus' death. Before dying, Jesus handed over the Spirit. After his death, water (the symbol of the Spirit)   `Jn 19:30, 34`

water and blood, Jesus Christ, not by water alone, but by water and blood. The Spirit is the one that testifies, and the Spirit is truth. [7]So there are three that testify, [8]the Spirit, the water, and the blood, and the three are of one accord. [9]If we accept human testimony, the testimony of God is surely greater. Now the testimony of God is this, that he has testified on behalf of his Son. [10]Whoever believes in the Son of God has this testimony within himself. Whoever does not believe God has made him a liar by not believing the testimony God has given about his Son.

[11]And this is the testimony: God gave us eternal life, and this life is in his Son. [12]Whoever possesses the Son has life; whoever does not possess the Son of God does not have life.

IV: EPILOGUE

Prayer for Sinners. [13]I write these things to you so that you may know that you have eternal life, you who believe in the name of the Son of God. [14]And we have this confidence in him, that if we ask anything according to his will, he hears us. [15]And if we know that he hears us in

flowed from his side, mingled with the blood he had shed salvifically. The secessionists may be placing all emphasis on Jesus' baptism (water), in which the Spirit descended on him, as the salvific coming; our author insists on the death (as well). (A
7-8 longer text of 6-8 reads: "So that there are three that testify *in heaven: Father, Word, and Holy Spirit; and these three are one; and there are three that testify on earth:* the Spirit, the water, and the blood; and the three are of one accord." The italicized words are the Johannine Comma [comma is part of a sentence]. Although missing from the Greek and Oriental textual witnesses, they appear among Latin writers in North Africa and Spain in the third century as a dogmatic reflection on and expansion of the "three that testify": "the Spirit" is the Father [Jn 4:24]; "the blood" is the Son; "the water" is the Spirit [Jn 7:38-39].) Basically First John is returning to the idea that the Spirit, present in the Christian through baptism, is the supreme witness to Jesus, the object of our faith. But in these verses emphasis is placed on the source of the Spirit, namely, Jesus glorified through death. Read in a Christian context, the author may be reminding his children that baptism and the eucharist testify to their faith in Jesus, as well as nourish it.

1 Jn 3:24; 4:13

Cf. Jn 7:38-39

Jn 1:31, 33

#3b?

9 The chief witness to Jesus (who is the truth) is the Spirit (who as the Spirit of Jesus is also the Spirit of truth) whom the Father has sent to give testimony about his Son. (Others see in "the testimony of God" a fourth and final witness to be added to the three above.) The divine witness, the Spirit, is the most convincing witness possible because through indwelling he becomes part of the believer. The ultimate blasphemy
11-12 is to reject this divine witness as false. The object of the divine testimony is Jesus, the incarnate Son, our life.

Jn 14:16-17; 16:13-14; 15:26

Cf. Jn 5:31-39

Mk 3:29

Jn 1:4; 11:25-26

regard to whatever we ask, we know that what we have asked him for is ours. ¹⁶If anyone sees his brother sinning, if the sin is not deadly, he should pray to God and he will give him life. This is only for those whose sin is not deadly. There is such a thing as deadly sin, about which I do not say that you should pray. ¹⁷All wrongdoing is sin, but there is sin that is not deadly.

¹⁸We know that no one begotten by God sins; but the one begotten by God he protects, and the evil one cannot touch him. ¹⁹We know that we belong to God, and the whole world is under the power of the evil one. ²⁰We also know that the Son of God has come and has given us discernment to know the one who is true. And we are in the one who is true, in his Son Jesus Christ. He is the true God and eternal life. ²¹Children, be on your guard against idols.

CONCLUSION

1 Jn 5:13-21

To assure his children that they share in this divine life has been the purpose of First John, the same basic purpose found in John—both writings state this in a conclusion. The theme of asking for things according to God's will (the Father's or the Son's?) returns again; but we should notice the limitation about agreement with God's will. The early church soon discovered that private requests were not always granted. One praiseworthy object of this Christian power of prayer is for brethren who have fallen into sin. Here, however, First John is cautious. For most sins, the prayer will be heard; but there is a sin so serious that John does not encourage prayer for it. Evidently the readers of the letter knew all about this sin. We are not so well informed (except that we should avoid identifying "sin unto death" with mortal sin, and "a sin *not* unto death" with venial sin). Probably the sin for First John was joining the secession, which was a form of apostasy, a sin elsewhere judged harshly.

But, lest there be any encouragement for laxity from the fact that forgiveness for most sins is obtainable through prayer, our author returns once more to the opposition between sin and being God's child. (In v. 18 some manuscripts read "is protected" or "protects himself.") Jesus, the Son of God, protects Christians from the devil; and so the children of God stand divided from Satan's world. There is in vv. 18-20 a series of three "We know" statements, defiant proclamations against the inroads of the secessionists. The last "We know" triumphantly confesses the coming of the Son of God, the acceptance of his revelation, and the consequent union with the Father through the Son. The "He is the true God" may refer

Jn 20:31
1 Jn 3:22;
Jn 16:24;
Mk 11:24

Heb 6:4-6;
10:26

1 Jn 3:8-9

Cf. Jn 3:11

14-15
16-17
18
19
20

to the Father or the Son, probably the latter, in which case First John ends, as John does, with a clear statement of the divinity of Jesus. Notice too that the theme of life which we met in the prologue of First John is again mentioned. The last words are a warning cried out in parting to the Johannine Christians, presumably against secession, for those who have gone out professing a false christology have gone over to idols—a term used elsewhere for false teaching.

Cf. Jn 20:28

#4

Ap 2:14, 20; 9:20

21

The Second Epistle of John

Text and Commentary

¹The Presbyter to the chosen Lady and to her children whom I love in truth—and not only I but also all who know the truth—²because of the truth that dwells in us and will be with us forever. ³Grace, mercy, and peace will be with us from God the Father and from Jesus Christ the Father's Son in truth and love.

⁴I rejoiced greatly to find some of your children walking in the truth just as we were commanded by the Father. ⁵But now, Lady, I ask you, not as though I were writing a new commandment but the one we have had from the beginning: let us love one another. ⁶For this is love,

that we walk according to his commandments; this is the commandment, as you heard from the beginning, in which you should walk.

⁷Many deceivers have gone out into the world, those who do not acknowledge Jesus Christ as coming in the flesh; such is the deceitful one and the antichrist. ⁸Look to yourselves that you do not lose what we worked for but may receive a full recompense. ⁹Anyone who is so "progressive" as not to remain in the teaching of the Christ does not have God; whoever remains in the teaching has the Father and the Son. ¹⁰If anyone comes to

1-2 Second John, unlike First John, has a title indicating the sender and the recipient. "The Elect [or Chosen] Lady" is a figure of speech for an unnamed local church and its members ("children"), a church within the presbyter's sphere of influence. Cf. p. 107 The presbyter loves this community in the divine truth (i.e., Jn 14:6
3 Jesus Christ) which abides in Christians. The greeting he gives Col 1:2; is the customary one for a Christian letter, with the Johannine 1 Tim 1:2 addition of "truth and love."

4 The presbyter compliments the church that at least some are "walking in truth" (the equivalent of "walking in light"; both 1 Jn 1:7
5 expressions are found in the Dead Sea Scrolls). The command-
6 ment of love is familiarly Johannine, as is the necessity of 1 Jn 2:7-8
7 living by the commandments. The source of trouble in the 1 Jn 2:3-5; 3:23; 4:1-3 church seems to be the same type of error found in First John.
8-9 Adoption of such error will deprive the Christians of the reward of eternal life that the presbyter has worked for. True 1 Jn 2:25 belief in Jesus is essential to any real worship of the Father, 1 Jn 2:23 so that the ultimate criterion for Christians is to remain in the traditional teaching of Christ (by him or about him?). The false 1 Jn 2:24; 2 Cor 11:4
10-11 teachers are to be rejected (a concept of heresy—a teaching so false it broke the *koinōnia* or fellowship—was now developing).

you and does not bring this doctrine, do not receive him in your house or even greet him; [11]for whoever greets him shares in his evil works.

[12]Although I have much to write to you, I do not intend to use paper and ink. Instead, I hope to visit you and to speak face to face so that our joy may be complete. [13]The children of your chosen sister send you greetings.

12-13   The letter finishes with a touch with which we are all familiar: an apology for the brevity of what we have written. Greetings are extended from a sister Christian church (probably that from which the presbyter is writing).

The Third Epistle of John

Text and Commentary

¹The Presbyter to the beloved Gaius whom I love in truth.

²Beloved, I hope you are prospering in every respect and are in good health, just as your soul is prospering. ³I rejoiced greatly when some of the brothers came and testified to how truly you walk in the truth. ⁴Nothing gives me greater joy than to hear that my children are walking in the truth.

⁵Beloved, you are faithful in all you do for the brothers, especially for strangers; ⁶they have testified to your love before the church. Please help them in a way worthy of God to continue their journey.

⁷For they have set out for the sake of the Name and are accepting nothing from the pagans. ⁸Therefore, we ought to support such persons, so that we may be co-workers in the truth.

⁹I wrote to the church, but Diotrephes, who loves to dominate, does not acknowledge us. ¹⁰Therefore, if I come, I will draw attention to what he is doing, spreading evil nonsense about us. And not content with that, he will not receive the brothers, hindering those who wish to do so and expelling them from the church.

¹¹Beloved, do not imitate evil but imi-

1   Third John also opens by naming the sender and the recipient (the briefest opening in a New Testament epistle, but characteristic of secular letters of the time). We know nothing of Gaius; he seems to be a layman although a later tradition **2-5**   would make him bishop of Pergamum. Gaius is blessed because some of the Christians have reported his kindness to **6-8**   travelling missionaries. We get a picture here of the early preachers of Christ, careful to reject aid from the pagans, depending on what was given them as an expression of brotherly charity by the Christians. The opportunity to support them by helping their journey is an opportunity to be a co-worker in the truth. Notice in these verses typical Johannine features, e.g., the emphasis on truth (1, 3, 8); "walking in truth" (4); the Name (7); brotherly love (5, 6).

9-10   A certain Diotrephes ignores the authority of the presbyter. He rejects the presbyter's letter (unknown to us), reviles him and blocks his missionaries. No heresy seems to be involved, just insubordination by an ambitious official, probably in Gaius' church or one nearby ("church" does not appear otherwise in the Fourth Gospel or in First and Second John). Diotrephes has some authority in casting people out of the church, **11**   and may have been a bishop. The presbyter applies to him the

tate good. Whoever does what is good is of God; whoever does what is evil has never seen God. [12]Demetrius receives a good report from all, even from the truth itself. We give our testimonial as well, and you know our testimony is true.

[13]I have much to write to you, but I do not wish to write with pen and ink. [14]Instead, I hope to see you soon, when we can talk face to face. [15]Peace be with you. The friends greet you; greet the friends there each by name.

12   test of the good and bad fruit. (However, the issue may actually be one of practical church structure—an issue in which subsequent history may have supported Diotrephes rather than the presbyter.) The same test is of happier outcome when applied to Demetrius (by later tradition bishop of Philadelphia). Demetrius is probably one of the missionaries for whom the letter acts as a recommendation before Gaius. In Demetrius' case, the truth itself (his Christian way of life?) recommends

13-15 him. The ending is the same as for Second John, with the added salutation of peace and good wishes. We might notice that Second John and Third John are of the same length, probably just enough to fill one papyrus sheet.

LECTIONARY READINGS FROM THE GOSPEL OF JOHN

1:1-18 Mass During the Day, Christmas

Seventh Day in the Octave of Christmas, December 31

Christian Initiation Apart from the Easter Vigil

1:6-8, 19-28 Third Sunday of Advent (B)

1:19-28 January 2

1:29-34 Second Sunday in Ordinary Time (A)

January 3

Christian Initiation Apart from the Easter Vigil

1:35-42 Second Sunday in Ordinary Time (B)

January 4

Christian Initiation: Entrance into the Order of Catechumens

Admission to Candidacy for Ordination as Deacons and Priests

1:35-51 For Priestly and Religious Vocations

1:43-51 January 5

1:45-51 August 24, St. Bartholomew, Apostle

Admission to Candidacy for Ordination as Deacons and Priests

1:47-51 September 29, SS. Michael, Gabriel, and Raphael, Archangels

2:1-11 Second Sunday in Ordinary Time (C)

January 7, if Epiphany is celebrated on January 7 or 8

February 11, Our Lady of Lourdes

Common of the Blessed Virgin Mary

Marriage

2:13-22 November 9, Dedication of St. John Lateran

Anniversary of the Dedication of a Church

2:13-25 Third Sunday of Lent (B)

3:1-6 Christian Initiation Apart from the Easter Vigil

Christian Initiation of Children

3:1-8 Monday, Second Week of Easter

3:7b-15 Tuesday, Second Week of Easter

3:13-17 September 14, Triumph of the Cross

3:14-21 Fourth Sunday of Lent (B)

3:16-18 Trinity Sunday (A)

3:16-21 Wednesday, Second Week of Easter

Christian Initiation Apart from the Easter Vigil

Reception of the Baptized into the Full Communion of the Church

3:22-30 January 12 or Saturday after Epiphany

3:31-36 Thursday, Second Week of Easter

4:5-14 Christian Initiation of Children

4:5-42 Third Sunday of Lent (A; optional B and C)

Third Week of Lent (optional)

4:19-24 Anniversary of the Dedication of a Church

Dedication of an Altar

4:43-54 Monday, Fourth Week of Lent

5:1-16 Tuesday, Fourth Week of Lent

5:17-30 Wednesday, Fourth Week of Lent

5:24-29 Masses for the Dead

5:31-47 Thursday, Fourth Week of Lent

5:33-36 Friday, Third Week of Advent

6:1-15 Seventeenth Sunday in Ordinary Time (B)

Friday, Second Week of Easter

Institution of Acolytes

Holy Eucharist

6:16-21 Saturday, Second Week of Easter

6:22-29 Monday, Third Week of Easter

6:24-35 Eighteenth Sunday in Ordinary Time (B)

Institution of Acolytes

Holy Eucharist

6:30-35 Tuesday, Third Week of Easter

6:35-40 Wednesday, Third Week of Easter

Anointing of the Sick

13:16-20 Thursday, Fourth Week of Easter
13:21-33, 36-38 Tuesday, Holy Week
13:31-33a, 34-35 Fifth Sunday of Easter (C)
14:1-6 Masses for the Dead
Friday, Fourth Week of Easter
14:1-12 Fifth Sunday of Easter (A)
14:6-14 May 3, SS. Philip and James, Apostles
Holy Name
14:7-14 Saturday, Fourth Week of Easter
14:15-21 Sixth Sunday of Easter (A)
14:15-17 Confirmation
14:15-16, 23b-26 Pentecost (C, optional)
14:15-23, 26-27 Reception of the Baptized into the Full Communion of the Church
14:21-26 Monday, Fifth Week of Easter
14:23-26 Confirmation
14:23-29 Sixth Sunday of Easter (C)
For a Council or Synod and Pastoral or Spiritual Meetings
For Peace and Justice
14:27-31a Tuesday, Fifth Week of Easter
15:1-6 Reception of the Baptized into the Full Communion of the Church
15:1-8 Fifth Sunday of Easter (B)
Wednesday, Fifth Week of Easter
February 21, St. Peter Damian, Bishop and Doctor of the Church
March 18, St. Cyril of Jerusalem, Bishop and Doctor of the Church
July 23, St. Bridget, Religious
October 15, St. Teresa of Jesus, Virgin and Doctor of the Church
November 16, St. Gertrude, Virgin
Common of Holy Men and Women

Consecration to a Life of Virginity and Religious Profession
For the Universal Church
For Religious
For the Laity
For the Sick
Sacred Heart (Votive Mass)
15:1-11 Christian Initiation Apart from the Easter Vigil
15:9-11 Thursday, Fifth Week of Easter
15:9-12 Marriage
For the Nation (State) or City, For Those Who Serve in Public Office, For the Assembly of National Leaders, For the King or Head of State, For the Progress of Peoples
15:9-17 Sixth Sunday of Easter (B)
January 24, St. Francis de Sales, Bishop and Doctor of the Church
March 4, St. Casimir
May 14, St. Matthias, Apostle
July 14, St. Camillus de Lellis, Priest
December 11, St. Damasus, Pope
Common of Pastors
Common of Holy Men and Women
Holy Orders
Consecration to a Life of Virginity and Religious Profession
For the Election of a Pope or Bishop
For Priests
For Priestly and Religious Vocations
In Thanksgiving
Sacred Heart (Votive Mass)
15:12-16 Marriage
15:12-17 Friday, Fifth Week of Easter
For Charity, For Promoting Harmony, For Relatives and Friends
15:18-21 Saturday, Fifth Week of Easter
February 23, St. Polycarp, Bishop and Martyr
April 13, St. Martin I, Pope

and Martyr
August 13, St. Pontian, Pope and Martyr, and Hippolytus, Priest and Martyr
Common of Martyrs
For the Laity

15:18-21, 26-27 Confirmation

15:18-21, 26–16:4 For Persecuted Christians

15:26–16:4a Monday, Sixth Week of Easter

15:26-27; 16:12-15 Pentecost (B, optional)

16:5-11 Tuesday, Sixth Week of Easter

16:5b-7, 12-13a Confirmation

16:12-15 Trinity Sunday (C)
Wednesday, Sixth Week of Easter

16:16-20 Thursday, Sixth Week of Easter

16:20-22 In Thanksgiving

16:20-23a Friday, Sixth Week of Easter

16:23b-28 Saturday, Sixth Week of Easter

16:29-33 Monday, Seventh Week of Easter

17:1-11a Seventh Sunday of Easter (A)
Tuesday, Seventh Week of Easter
For Unity of Christians

17:6, 14-19 Holy Orders

17:11b-19 Seventh Sunday of Easter (B)
Wednesday, Seventh Week of Easter
April 11, St. Stanislaus, Bishop and Martyr
June 2, SS. Marcellinus and Peter, Martyrs
September 16, SS. Cornelius, Pope and Martyr, and Cyprian, Bishop and Martyr
Common of Martyrs
For Unity of Christians
For Persecuted Christians

17:11b, For the Universal Church

17-23 For the Election of a Pope or Bishop
For the Spread of the Gospel

17:20-26 Seventh Sunday of Easter (C)
Thursday, Seventh Week of Easter
April 24, St. Fidelis of Sigmaringen, Priest and Martyr
May 26, St. Philip Neri, Priest
June 28, St. Irenaeus, Bishop and Martyr
August 20, St. Bernard, Abbot and Doctor of the Church
November 12, St. Josaphat, Bishop and Martyr
Common of Holy Men and Women
Marriage
Consecration to a Life of Virginity and Religious Profession
For Unity of Christians
Sacred Heart (Votive Mass)

17:24-26 Masses for the Dead

18:1-19:42 Good Friday

18:33b-37 Christ the King (B)

19:17-18, 25-39 Masses for the Dead

19:25-27 September 15, Our Lady of Sorrows
Common of the Blessed Virgin Mary
Votive Mass of the Blessed Virgin Mary

19:25-30 Burial of Baptized Children
Burial of Non-baptized Children

19:28-37 Holy Cross

19:31-35 Christian Initiation of Children

19:31-37 Solemnity of the Sacred Heart (B)
Holy Eucharist
Precious Blood
Sacred Heart (Votive Mass)

20:1-9 Easter Sunday

20:1-2, 11-18 July 22, St. Mary Magdalene

20:2-8 December 27, St. John, Apostle and Evangelist

20:11-18 Tuesday, Octave of Easter
20:19-23 Pentecost
     Holy Orders
     For Peace and Justice
20:19-31 Second Sunday of Easter
20:24-29 July 3, St. Thomas, Apostle
21:1-14 Friday, Octave of Easter
     Institution of Acolytes
     Holy Eucharist
21:1-19 Third Sunday of Easter (C)
21:15-17 January 20, St. Fabian, Pope
     and Martyr

April 30, St. Pius V, Pope
August 21, St. Pius X, Pope
     Common of Pastors
     Holy Orders
     For the Universal Church
     For Priests
21:15-19 Friday, Seventh Week of Easter
     June 29, SS. Peter and Paul,
     Apostles
21:20-25 Saturday, Seventh Week of
     Easter

LECTIONARY READINGS FROM 1 JOHN

1:1-4 December 27, St. John, Apostle and Evangelist
     Institution of Readers
1:5–2:2 April 29, St. Catherine of Siena, Virgin and Doctor of the Church
     December 28, Holy Innocents, Martyrs
     For Forgiveness of Sins
2:1-5a Third Sunday of Easter (B)
2:1-5 For Reconciliation
2:3-11 December 29, Fifth Day in the Octave of Christmas
2:12-17 December 30, Sixth Day in the Octave of Christmas
2:18-21 December 31, Seventh Day in the Octave of Christmas
2:18-25 January 13, St. Hilary, Bishop and Doctor of the Church
2:22-28 January 2
2:29–3:6 January 3
3:1-2 Fourth Sunday of Easter (B)
     Anointing of the Sick
     Masses for the Dead
3:1-3 November 1, All Saints
3:1-2, 21-24 Holy Family (C, optional)
3:7-10 January 4
3:11-21 January 5
3:14-16 Masses for the Dead
3:14-18 March 8, St. John of God, Religious
     July 4, St. Elizabeth of Portugal
     July 14, St. Camillus de Lellis, Priest

November 17, St. Elizabeth of Hungary, Religious
     Common of Holy Men and Women
     For Charity, For Promoting Harmony, For Relatives and Friends
3:18-24 Fifth Sunday of Easter (B)
     Marriage
3:22–4:6 January 7 or Monday after Epiphany
4:7-10 Sixth Sunday of Easter (B)
     January 8 or Tuesday after Epiphany
     Solemnity of the Sacred Heart (A)
4:7-16 July 29, St. Martha
     August 28, St. Augustine, Bishop and Doctor of the Church
     Common of Holy Men and Women
     Consecration to a Life of Virginity and Religious Profession
     Sacred Heart (Votive Mass)
4:7-12 Marriage
4:9-15 For Unity of Christians
4:11-16 Seventh Sunday of Easter (B)
4:11-18 January 9 or Wednesday after Epiphany
4:19–5:4 January 10 or Thursday after Epiphany
5:1-5 March 18, St. Cyril of Jerusalem, Bishop and Doctor of the Church

May 2, St. Athanasius, Bishop and Doctor of the Church

June 21, St. Aloysius Gonzaga, Religious

August 2, St. Eusebius of Vercelli, Bishop

Common of Martyrs

Common of Holy Men and Women

5:1-6 Second Sunday of Easter (B)

5:1-9 Baptism of the Lord (B, optional)

5:4-8 Holy Eucharist
Precious Blood

5:5-13 January 6 (in countries where Epiphany is celebrated on January 7 or 8)
January 11 or Friday after Epiphany

5:14-21 January 7 (in countries where Epiphany is celebrated on January 7 or 8)
January 12 or Saturday after Epiphany

LECTIONARY READINGS FROM 2 JOHN

4-9 Friday in the Thirty-second Week of Ordinary Time (Year II)

LECTIONARY READINGS FROM 3 JOHN

5-8 Saturday in the Thirty-second Week of Ordinary Time (Year II)

REVIEW AIDS AND DISCUSSION TOPICS

I

Introduction to the Gospel according to John (pages 9–19)

1. How has the original text of John been established? Why is the concise form of a text sometimes the oldest? Do most scholars agree with St. Irenaeus' statement that John, son of Zebedee, was the beloved disciple and/or author of the Gospel? Was he the author of the Apocalypse and the Epistles?

2. When was the Fourth Gospel written? Was the author familiar with the other three Gospels? Give examples that prove that John stressed events in Jesus' life that foreshadowed the sacramental life of the church.

3. How do the four Gospels compare with one another? How have the Qumran and Chenoboskion documents contributed to an understanding of Johannine sources?

4. Give the general plan and major subdivisions of the Fourth Gospel.

5. State eight Johannine characteristics. Illustrate each of these characteristics with examples from the Gospel.

II

The Prologue, The First Week, New Institutions (pages 21–39)

1. Show that the prologue is a poetic summary of the whole theology and narrative of the Gospel, as well as an introduction. Quote the verses that refer to Genesis, to the rejection of Jesus, to his acceptance and to the new covenant.

2. According to John, what did Jesus accomplish on the first five days after the Baptist's testimony? Show that John the Baptist is "the first witness" in the trial of Jesus. Is there a complete christology in the words of John the Baptist? Can we find a timelessly true portrait of vocation in the calling of the first disciples?

3. Give two examples of "inclusion" in the wedding at Cana. Explain Jesus' words to his mother. Discuss this "miraculous sign" in relation to messianism and the sacraments. How did the first sign affect the religious development of the disciples?

4. Show how the three incidents of the miracle at Cana, the cleansing of the Temple, the conversation with Nicodemus teach us that Jesus came to replace Jewish purifications, the Temple, and birth into the Chosen People.

5. How does the conversation of Jesus and the Samaritan woman follow the typical instruction pattern of Johannine misunderstanding? What three great equations does John teach us? Contrast the three miracles about the son or servant boy (Jn 4:43-54; Mt 8:5-13; Lk 7:1-10).

III

Replacing the Feasts of "the Jews" (pages 39–61)

1. Describe the scene at Bethesda and show how Jesus, the new Moses, replaces the Sabbath ordinance. Name the four witnesses he cites to support his claim. Will the Pharisees accept these witnesses?

2. Study the miracle of the multiplication of the loaves and fishes as recorded by each of the four evangelists. Which of the Synoptics offers practically the same sequence of events as does John? What does Jesus teach about the manna, the bread of life, the eucharist?

3. Describe the ceremonies of the feast of Tabernacles. Did Jesus contradict himself when he went up to Jerusalem? What did he teach on this occasion about the source of living water, the light of the world, the meaning of the water and light ceremonies?

4. Contrast the story of the adulteress and the dilemma connected with Caesar's coin. Trace the theme of life in chapters 2–4 and 5–7. Show that the theme of light that is developed in chapters 8–10 is centered on the healing of the blind in chapter 9.

5. What was the origin of the feast of Dedication (or Hanukkah)? What great lesson does Jesus teach about himself on this occasion?

IV

From Death to Life and from Life to Death (pages 61–70)

1. Why does it seem possible that John's report of the public ministry of Jesus may have ended with chapter 10? How does the theme of the raising of Lazarus (chapters 11–12) supply a transition between the Jordan and Jerusalem and prepare for the events leading to Jesus' death?

2. Show how the raising of Lazarus is a fitting conclusion to the Book of Signs and a fitting introduction to the Book of Glory. What do we know about Lazarus, Mary, Martha, Bethany? Is there any solid basis for identifying Mary of Bethany with the Galilean sinner or Mary of Magdala?

3. In the story of Lazarus find examples of misunderstanding, irony, double meaning, inclusion, realized eschatology, duplicate speeches, and rearrangement in relation to the Synoptic order.

4. What time indications does John give in chapters 11–12? Clarify the relationship between the different anointing stories. Explain the significant differences between John's account of the "Palm Sunday" procession and those of the Synoptics.

5. What comment does John make on the failure of Jesus' own to receive him? How is 11:44-50 a fine summary of Jesus' message to the world? Most of these ideas are found elsewhere in John. Where?

V

The Last Discourse: Part One (pages 71–82)

1. What is the real meaning of the foot-washing scene? Is there an underlying sacramental motif? Discuss the time indication given by John for the Last Supper: "Before the feast of the Passover."

2. What is the best explanation of the words: "Whoever has *bathed* has no need except to have his feet washed, for he is clean all over"? Where can we find a place for the institution of the eucharist in John's Last Supper?

3. Show that the Last Supper as recorded by John has Passover characteristics. Describe the roles of Peter and the beloved disciple in the betrayal account. Explain the peculiar reference to "heel" in 12:18.

4. Give examples of the atemporal and aspatial character of the Last Discourse. How does Jesus answer the difficulties proposed by Thomas and Philip?

5. Show how the theme is applied that, if we keep the commandments, the Paraclete-Spirit (14:15-17), the Son (14:18-22), and the Father (14:23-24) will come to dwell with us. What does Jesus teach here about the coming of the Spirit? Analyze the duplicate of the first part of the discourse in 16:4-33.

VI

The Last Discourse: Part Two and Three (pages 82–87)

1. Explain the metaphor of the vine and the branches. What is the Old Testament meaning of vine and vineyard? Will the vine of the New Israel ever be uprooted? Explain how Jesus as vine is another echo of Jesus as divine wisdom.

2. How are the themes of divine indwelling, asking in Jesus' name, keeping the commandments (which were treated in the first part of the discourse) repeated here?

3. Why will the true disciples of Jesus always be hated? Why does the injustice of the world's hatred call for the services of the Paraclete?

4. Drawing a parallel from the Mass, discuss the "Priestly Prayer" of chapter 17 as "the preface to the historical and eternally valid offering of the cross." What echoes are to be found here of the "Our Father"?

5. What petitions does Jesus make for his disciples and for all believers? On what note of triumph does Jesus end his prayer?

VII

Passion, Death, Resurrection, and Ascension (pages 87–104)

1. What does John relate about the garden scene and the inquiry before Annas? Correlate these facts with the accounts given by the Synoptics.

2. How do the seven scenes of the trial reveal its real meaning? Describe each scene. According to John: (a) Did "the Jews" want execution by crucifixion? (b) What is the difference between the Gentile political understanding of kingship of the Jews and the Jewish religious understanding? (c) Who was Barabbas? (d) When was Jesus scourged and mocked? (e) How often did Pilate say Jesus was not guilty? (f) Why did Jesus remain silent? (g) Why did Pilate yield?

3. How many references to the Passover are to be found in John's passion narrative? List the details of the crucifixion given by the Synoptics and omitted by John. Discuss the significance of Jesus' words to his mother in the light of the Cana incident and the Garden of Eden. Explain why Augustine saw in the water and blood flowing from Jesus' side the fundamental Christian sacraments of baptism and the eucharist.

4. Discuss the differing details of the various resurrection appearances. Describe the Jerusalem appearances as recorded by John. On what note does chapter 20 close?

5. Is chapter 21 supplementary to John's Gospel? What incidents does it contain? Have these incidents Johannine characteristics? On what note does chapter 21 close?

VIII

The Johannine Epistles: Introduction and Commentary (*pages* 105–126)

1. Are the Johannine Epistles to be attributed to the author of the Gospel? Was First John written before or after the Gospel? On what occasion was it written? How is it divided? Are Second and Third John by the author of First John?

2. Compare the prologue of First John with that of the Gospel. What does this epistle teach about light, sin, commandments, opposition to the world, antichrists?

3. How does the author of First John teach his readers to walk as children of the God of love (1 Jn 3:11–4:6)?

4. What does he teach about love and faith (1 Jn 4:7–5:12)? Quote and explain the Johannine Comma. How does he conclude this letter?

5. Summarize the lessons of Second and Third John. List the Johannine themes these letters contain.

Other works of Raymond E. Brown published by The Liturgical Press:

A Coming Christ in Advent
  (Essays on the Gospel Narratives Preparing for the Birth of Jesus—
  Matthew 1 and Luke 1)

An Adult Christ at Christmas
  (Essays on the Three Biblical Christmas Stories—
  Matthew 2 and Luke 2)

A Crucified Christ in Holy Week
  (Essays on the Four Gospel Passion Narratives)